Thoughts from a Queen-Sized Bed

American Lives
series editor: Tobias Wolff

Thoughts from a Queen-Sized Bed

For Frieda,

Mimi Schwartz

Mimi Schwartz

University of Nebraska Press / *Lincoln and London*

Acknowledgments for the use of previously published
material appear on page 158–59.

∞

Library of Congress Cataloging-in-Publication Data
Schwartz, Mimi.
Thoughts from a queen-sized bed / Mimi Schwartz.
p. cm.
ISBN 0-8032-4294-8 (cloth: alk. paper)
1. Schwartz, Mimi. 2. English teachers—United States—Biography. 3. Married
women—United States—Biography. 4. Jewish women—United States—Biography.
5. Jewish families—United States. 6. Marriage—United States. I. Title.
PE64.S38 A3 2002
428'.0092—dc21
[B]
2001033593

"N"

Designed and composed by
Todd Duren of Firefly Design. Set in New Caledonia
and Suburban fonts.

For Stu, and our shared bed

Contents

PART 3: LIFE AFTER BREAKFAST

4 A.M. Preface

I am lying in bed, watching white vines climb pale blue walls as they have, day and night, ever since we bought this house with its indestructible wallpaper. Thirty-one years and not a ripple, a bump, a tear, as if we'd just moved in. I imagine a full moon out there behind the room-darkening shades, its shine a soft stage light making papered vines dance in shadow. I imagine crisp stars, Orion's belt touching the tops of cherry trees lining our side of the street.

Beside me, Stu, my husband of forty years, is snoring, not his loud sitcom snores but soft rhythmic sighs trying to be reasonable. I wrap myself around him for comfort but am too hot to stay this way unless I fall asleep in minutes. The goose-down comforter ordered by catalog as "summer weight" is a fake—it's as hot as the old one—and I sweat even with a window open two inches in February. My husband resists this nightly air and wears flannel pajamas in revenge; I, naked, want to feel his skin.

If we had a king-sized bed, or twin beds, or slept in separate rooms, I would have more space to be restless. I could put on a light, read. In my daughter's old room, I could dial old boyfriends from last night's dreams. If I were out of town, I could throw off all covers, take a noisy bath, and sprawl across the bed, unrestrained, in a Marriott or Hyatt silence that lets me sleep but then wakes me, as if I had lost something essential.

I turn my pillow to the cold side and roll toward the weight that pulls me to the center of the bed. I do not listen, as I did in childhood, for footsteps climbing old stairs of fear to get me. I do not run my fingers up and down a papered seam, wishing that yellow rosebuds were warriors with swords drawn.

The dogwood branches scrape the window panes, and I whisper, "Turn over," because my husband is now on his back and I have nothing to hold on to. He moans, obeys, and I press against his butt and spine, focusing on his breathing, in and out, in and out, until his rhythm becomes mine, and I doze for another half-hour.

The essays in this book began in this bed fifteen years ago. They are the thoughts between dozing and waking that rouse me like a soldier hearing gunshots, so I can't retreat back to sleep. Decisions about moths in the closet, what is in the freezer, and who will sew on buttons demand 2 A.M. resolution. So do the 3 A.M. echoes of family stories that I grew up on. How to survive, how to be true to myself, what is beautiful, what is love, all seem imbedded in memory and collective expectations that shaped who I was supposed to become. And whether I embrace or resist these legacies, they leave their mark, forcing me to find my niche between parents who valued sacrifice and obligation and children who pursue freedom and self-realization.

Bodies disappoint us; we will not live forever; parents cannot protect us; we are getting fat. Yes, yes, I know all that but . . . , I say before daybreak, getting out of bed to write down game plans before I forget them and they disappear into air.

"Where are you going?" Stu asks, putting his face two inches from his alarm clock so he could read 5:03 A.M. in white digitals.

"Into my study."

"Wake me at seven, and I'll warm you up," he says, as I put on socks so my feet don't get numb beside the lukewarm heating grates that have just kicked on.

Part 1: Midnight to 5 A.M.

Front Door on the Driveway

My father bought the house in 1941, the story goes, to get out of Jackson Heights, Queens, New York. I was six months old, and he wanted a real house, not a three-room walk-up in a row house of relatives, his brother's family above him. A Dutch Colonial, two towns away in Forest Hills, a few blocks from a family he had known in Germany, seemed perfect—especially for the new baby, ME, the first Yankee in the family. They would rent it, he told the realtor, who said it could be bought for a song because of a foreclosure. Three hours and a fifty-dollar deposit later, my dad got a phone call notifying him that he'd won the bid and owned a house. "But we didn't even see the basement or top floor," my mother said, as they each broke out in a cold sweat. They were Americans now, like it or not.

A bad mistake, a crazy house, I thought for the next eighteen years, because to find us you had to walk off 110th Street onto a narrow cement driveway and make a sharp left twenty yards later, up four brick steps to the "front" porch. It was built to overlook 70th Road, but by the time my parents moved in, right after Pearl Harbor was bombed, our only view was of a high hemlock hedge separating us from the boxy house next door.

We never knew that neighbor, except that she was a squat woman with burnt-red hair and crucifix earrings who gave only two Hershey kisses on Halloween. We did know the Levskys, whose house abutted my bedroom window and whose huge black dog bit me once when I was playing with their son, Bobby. His mom had bleached hair, of which my mother didn't approve, but Bobby and I set up a bedroom phone line with string and paper cups anyway.

And we knew the Goldsmiths across the street, whose varsity-all-star son loved my sister and whose daughter, Arlene, had Shirley Temple curls, dimples, blue eyes, and argyle sweaters—all things I wanted and couldn't have, except for the argyle sweater, which my mother copied for me.

She was an expert knitter, so good that she landed the first American job of the family before she reached Ellis Island. A Mr. Fredericks, so the story goes, had been on their boat, traveling home from a hat-buying trip in Europe, and spotted my two sisters, Ruth and Hannah, wearing matching knit hats and coats, which my mother had designed; he hired her on the spot. So while my father and his two brothers tried to restart a leather business in America, my mother, aunts, and grandmother were knitting slippers, hats, and booties from morning to night. Three years later J. F. Hats wanted my mother as a full-time designer, but my father "wouldn't hear of it" because I was about to be born. I didn't know this until, thirty years later, she told me over lunch, right before I started teaching at a college seventy miles away. "Weren't you resentful?" I asked. It was the late seventies, the women's movement was in high gear, and no one I knew was staying home just for kids. (Certainly no husband I knew was saying "Don't" out loud.) My mother shook her head. "You were enough," she said, smiling, as I squirmed.

The neighbors my parents liked were the Shulmans, who moved in behind us.† Educated people from Vienna, my dad said, and I should play with their children. I hated them, of course. The boy had glasses and wore a bow tie, and the girl had stringy brown hair, worse than mine, and read science books all day long. But even if they'd been my version of perfect, it wouldn't have mattered. I had enough foreignness at home and wasn't about to get more of it voluntarily. America was considered a melting pot then (multiculturalism was not even a word in the 1940s), and I wanted to jump right in. The more I was urged to play with the Schulman kids, the more I went over to P.S. 3 with Bobby and Arlene and some kids from 108th Street to flip for picture trading cards of Blue Boy and Pink Lady in fancy, courtly clothes. Strictly American.

I was just as resistant to Dr. Schmidt, the dour-faced doctor, formerly from Berlin, who made house calls with his black bag and always gave his verdict, *sehr schlimm* (very, very bad), stroking his chin. And I was

---

† To protect the privacy of friends and relatives I've changed names and some locations, but the rest is true—as I see it.

a misery on family Sundays when all my aunts, uncles, and cousins would converge at someone's house to feast, plan leather strategies, and gossip, half in English, half in German, while we children whispered in a bedroom about menstruation or the sexy parties Cousin Dora had when her parents weren't home.

"Dora needs a good spanking!" my father would say on the way home when my sister demanded Ruby Passion nail polish or whatever delight Dora had on that week. "And Richard should take his head out of a book and talk more," my mother would add, while I defended him, the one older cousin who was nice to "the pipsqueak," me.

It was my sister Ruth who took on the serious training of a Teutonic father. The battles started when I was four and she was twelve and lasted until she married at nineteen. No, she couldn't wear lipstick. No, she couldn't stay out until midnight, or hang out at Penn Drug after Friday night basketball games, or go steady, or get pinned. Such goings on were unheard of in Germany, my father would shout in fury at least once a week, his face scarlet.

"But Dad, everyone else is . . ."

"You should date the Schulzberger boy. His mother is a Tannhauser and in Germany . . ."

"Dad, this is America!"

They would yell back and forth until a fist slammed on the table. Then angry footsteps would climb the stairs, and I would turn on the radio to *Stella Dallas* or *The Shadow*. Someday, I'd vow, I would date the boys *I* wanted to date, and to hell with my father. Fortunately he'd mellowed by the time I met a boy in bio lab, who had broad shoulders, sexy lips, and parents who came from Russia, via Brooklyn, to Burns Street, across the boulevard from us. And when, six years later, I married this boy named Stu, by then an engineer on his way to California to shoot Ranger rockets to the Moon, my dad was delighted. He finally had the son he'd missed in a house full of women—even if he couldn't recite the parents' genealogy.

There was one thing, besides my mother's raspberry Linzer torte, that I did like about being the child of Jews from Germany: the survival stories. Every weekend my dad, who needed to walk because of his heart, would go up and down the sidewalks of Forest Hills with me, telling me how the family had left Germany, how he and his brothers had outwitted the Nazis and landed us safely in Queens. Their being heroes made me feel braver. But still I shivered during movie newsreels about children from Auschwitz, knowing I was safe only because my father had heard a drumbeat at a town square in Schwarzwald and knew what to do.

The year was 1933, Hitler was campaigning for election in the next town, and my father, who looked like a Prussian soldier with his "Aryan" blond hair and blue eyes, wanted to hear him speak. My mother was afraid, but my dad went anyway, arriving early to get a seat. He had already heard the drumbeats, which had started softly at dawn to call people to the rally and kept getting louder. By noon they were deafening, until Hitler appeared, and they stopped.

Sieg Heil, Sieg Heil, the crowd of thousands roared, rising in unison to salute. And my father rose, too, not out of fear, but in response to some hypnotic mass reflex that usurped his will. "I couldn't help myself," he told my mother that night and said they must leave Germany. "This man was too dangerous."

To emigrate to the United States you needed money or a rich sponsor, which he didn't have. So for three years my dad and his brothers used the language of the leather trade to smuggle out their capital. The price of cowhides and goatskins on the world market became a code for specifying behind which toilets, on which trains going from Frankfurt to Switzerland, their money would be taped. My dad, on the Swiss side of the border, would await his brothers' call, board the train, and find the envelopes of cash.

Ten or twelve trains later, the family had enough of a nest egg to start over in America. Three years after that, they were in Queens, and seven years later, my dad was walking with me, telling me all this. It taught me about the art of the possible, how if you were smart and brave and lucky, you could have happy endings in life, even if it meant changing countries just like that.

Curiously, in all our neighborhood travels, I never noticed the *other* house with the front door on the driveway. It was three blocks away, I found out, when a date got lost on my instructions and called me from its kitchen. I walked over to get him and, sure enough, there was an English Tudor with no apparent front door, just like ours.

I was disappointed. By then—the year was 1956—I had my saddle shoes, my plaid kilt skirts, my crew-neck sweaters to fit in, and felt American enough to enjoy being slightly out of cultural sync. I'd even made peace with the Oriental rugs, which I hated all through childhood. "My dad got them at the Persian bazaar when he traveled in his twenties," I'd tell friends who had the normal wall-to-wall carpets that I'd coveted for years.

In fact my parents' rugs are under my feet as I sit in my house in New Jersey, an old colonial with a big front porch, easy to see. After my father died, my mother moved to a carpeted apartment and, as our wood floors were bare, I took the rugs. I had missed the swirling scrolls (they weren't snakes, after all), and my children were pleased because their friends next-door, a Catholic family from New Orleans, had similar rugs. We like all the neighbors and see them every Labor Day at a potluck picnic. With the exception of Christmas, when the other windows have colored lights and we go skiing, we feel we fit in.

I still walk past my old house in Queens now and then. We find parking spots nearby when we come back to visit Stu's parents, who, once their two boys left, moved to a new high-rise apartment two blocks away. "I want everything new," Stu's mother, Rose, explained when Stu balked, as I did when my parents sold their house after I left for college. I wanted to keep my room, even if they were tired of the upstairs tub leaking into the front hall.

The house is still white, but the shutters keep changing with each new owner's whim. For years they'd been a hard, glossy black, and I kept looking for mean people to peek out of the windows. Then they were cranberry, and I rang the bell once to ask if I could see my old room, but no one answered. Now they are medium blue, like we had in the 1950s. The other day, when we passed by on our way back from a stuffed-cabbage dinner at Stu's parents', I saw a woman from India, or maybe Iran, with a dark veil, raising the Venetian blinds in the front den. Her eyes were black and solemn, she had a jeweled mark on her forehead, and I wondered, as she disappeared into the room, if *she* had daughters who went to Forest Hills High and necked to love songs in that room while she slept upstairs?

Jimmy and June

When I was fifteen and ready for love, my ideal couple was Jimmy Stewart and June Allyson, whatever their movie. He was a pilot, a bandleader, a ball player, and she, with her throaty voice and prim crinolines, was always there, urging him to glory.

They never squabbled, as my parents did every Sunday night, trying to decide whether the Grand Central Parkway or the Long Island Expressway would have less traffic going home. My dad would open his car door and say, "What do you think, Geddle?" and she, unfailingly, would give an answer, which twenty minutes later would be wrong. We'd sit bumper-to-bumper while he raged, she sulked, and I sat silently in the back seat, wondering why she didn't keep her mouth shut.

Whenever Stu says, "Which way should we go?" I'm no fool: "Whichever way you want, dear!" Of course that never stopped me from getting suckered into the stop-tailgating trap or the can't-you-ask-someone trap, which June and Jimmy never fell into because Jimmy, running late, never got furiously lost. And if he did, June never doubted him with clenched fists and her disloyal foot on the brake.

Our first knock-down-drag-out battle took place six months after our honeymoon, and I was shocked. We both were. It was my first cooking victory other than franks and beans or spaghetti, and I brought it to the table as if it were beef Wellington for King Louis. But new wife or not, Stu wasn't about to fake it.

"What's this?" He pulled away from the casserole as if it were the plague.

"Macaroni and cheese!" I beamed, heaping three scoops onto his plate. I was so into my accomplishment I didn't notice how the voice dropped, the shoulders hunched, the jaw set.

"I don't eat the stuff!" he said. "What else do you have?"

"Jake's Bar down the block, you jerk. I spent two hours on this. This is from scratch."

In a movie script—the fifties or now—you could expect the couple to start arguing, which we did, until macaroni flies around, which it did, and he storms out, which he did, and she cries on the speckled dinette table, which I did. She would then meet a macaroni-and-cheese lover in the supermarket, he would take up with his secretary, and ten years later they'd be split up or living together like zombies. Which we never did.

Many, many years later, when the mood strikes, I still try culinary coups, but now when Stu's shoulders slump, I know the signs. So I ask, "Do you like it?" until he admits there's too much salt or steamed eggplant is not his favorite. Then I am silent until he gets mad, and we fight over something safe like who forgot to go to the cleaners. Someone storms out, and later we sleep on far sides of the bed until one of us wraps around the other in the middle of the night, pretending to be asleep.

The morning after their Sunday fiascoes, my father sang, my mother, who never smiled before her third cup of coffee, glowed, and I waited for divorce. Pre-macaroni, I didn't know that dumb, ritual fights were the subtext for the resentments that surface later—By the way, why *didn't* you call today? . . . Do you *have* to read *Newsweek* before we make love?—the ones that get answered in whispers, after fury and forgiveness, in each other's arms.

Jimmy and June were never that insecure or petty, just as they never shouted "Idiot!" or "Moron!" during a traffic jam. Their fights were about important things such as whether he should risk his life breaking through the sound barrier.

"But I need you," June would plead, trying to keep him safe, as the skies darkened and the music filled with fear.

"And I need you," Jimmy would answer, going off anyway. June, waving bravely, didn't sulk like my mother. Nor would I, I'd vow, eating popcorn with my friends in the Midway balcony. Love meant decorum.

"All happy families are alike; but each unhappy family is unhappy in its own way," I read, at twenty, in *Anna Karenina* and believed those lines as fully as I believed in fifties movies. I was about to be married and, like Tolstoy's Levin and Kitty, I had high expectations. I planned to be 100 percent happy, loyal, and committed because I had hooked "Mr. Right." I'd never become like my Aunt Sophie, who turned cheerful only after Uncle Kurt died.

I just reread *Anna Karenina* and realized that I have met no "happy families that are alike"—except on reruns of *The Brady Bunch* and

Ozzie and Harriet, legacies of Jimmy and June. The "happy" families I know, my own included, are just as complicated as those in misery. Some days you feel like a devoted June, some days like a trapped Anna, ready for a liberating passion even if it lands you under a moving train. Like Anna, your mind keeps clicking: Is a lover worth giving up everything for? But, unlike Anna, you're also wondering: Will he, in three years, be that much better than my husband?

The mood can last for weeks, even longer, but then, just when you think you must get out of this mess, some magic rehappens—"You Go to My Head," "Falling in Love with Love"—as on the old Frank Sinatra records stacked under the hi-fi. You lean toward each other for days, "I love you, you idiot," you joke and whisper, as if happily ever after is forever.

Maybe the magic is a mind-set. My father, at our wedding, toasted us with this caveat: "Before you get married ask, 'Will I be happy?' Afterward say, 'I *will* be happy.'" I didn't know what he was talking about. I was still thinking either/or. Either you were Jimmy and June or you weren't. I never expected "I love you, I hate you," to get all mixed up, part of one blended rhythm, hard to follow. Still, I kept telling myself I was happy—or would be again—if one more time I'd give him a backrub or he'd kiss my neck.

At a rose garden wedding last month, the pastor, who was a man under thirty, told the young couple before him: "Don't try to change one another. Rather grow toward each other."

"It took me twenty-five years to figure that out. How does he know that already?" I heard behind me. It was our old neighbors, the ones who battled so loudly and frequently that no one had given their marriage more than two years. That was twenty-eight years ago.

"I could have used that man at *my* wedding!" I said as we were walking out, our old neighbors behind us. I turned to chat.

"Wouldn't have mattered," Stu said, giving my back a poke. It was boiling in the sun, and he wanted me to keep moving toward the air-conditioned reception. "You would have given your pre-breakfast lectures, no matter what."

"Probably," I agreed, remembering my early crusades to change him—Be more spontaneous! Say may I, not can I! Don't be so groggy in the morning!—until the night of the macaroni, when his litany of my faults made dishes fly and walls shake. I'd been sure he adored me as I was and then discovered I was a nag, unorganized, never put my goddamn shoes away, talked nonstop about nonsense, especially in the morning, and was driving him crazy, especially with these burnt, creamy casseroles, the worst.

It had been great, *post*-macaroni, I remember. When he got back from the bar, we made passionate love. He'd missed me, he said. I'd missed him, I said—and I smiled the next morning, just like my mother. Of course, I kept working on perfecting him until Julie and Alan were born, and then I started working on them instead. But I kept a healthy respect for his blow-ups, which came with less intensity over the years *if* I kept quiet until after his third cup of coffee. So, pastor, you are right; we have learned to grow toward each other . . .

"I've been married ten times to the same woman," Stu likes to say, because our relationship keeps reinventing itself. The June Allyson housewife who spent hours on macaroni and cheese has switched to takeout sushi and stir-fry veggies that Stu chops with the Chinese cleaver I bought him last year for inspiration. Ten years ago he wasn't even boiling water. He had no time. He was a busy man, and I was supposed to do all that. He'd empty the dishwasher, delighted with his own generosity. I'd want to punch him for his smugness, but instead I'd instruct him on the stacking of plates.

"No wonder everything gets cracked!" I'd mutter.

"Then *you* stack them!" he'd yell.

"I do enough. My job is seventy-two miles from home!" I'd yell, glad to score a real point at last. "You're the one whose office is three blocks away."

"And that's where I'm going."

Doors slammed, dishes rattled, something may have cracked, but we used it anyway, whatever it was.

Maybe we've stayed together because when we think about moving, we renovate instead (we just refaced the bathtub and replaced the showerhead). Maybe it's because we both like ripped T-shirts and worn, comfortable shoes and eat the same Thanksgiving dishes with the same people every year. A former friend got rid of her split-level house, her lawyer husband, her brown hair, and her teaching job and moved far from everyone she knew. She never called, and she started a new life with no reminders. I admire her gutsiness but would feel lost and unconnected without reminders. Who I was and who I am need to be in the same rooms.

At times these rooms are dark, claustrophobic, the marriage walls closing in; but more often they are bright with memory and conversation, steeped in a shared history about a girl in khaki pants and long auburn hair who was stacked in tight sweaters, and a boy with broad shoulders and horn-rimmed glasses who planned to be the first man on the moon. That boy will have a heart attack one day; that girl, a mastectomy. Still we keep conjuring up old selves. I love you-of-my-Jones-Beach-midnight-swims-days, we say over and over, reaching for each other in the middle of the night when an ambulance siren moans or the wind howls. The comfort of each other's touch.

Maybe we stay together because when I see dying grass, he sees green; when he gets faint at the sight of blood, I get Band-Aids. Or because we both like peanut butter when we're on diets. He takes a little, then I take a little, then we grin in communal sin, vowing tomorrow will be different.

Or because our gold wedding bands, once grooved for subtlety, have become smooth, patternless, like the sheets on our bed after we straighten them together. "To get the wrinkles out of our marriage," Stu likes to say. And I see June smoothing the thinning percale sheets on his side, and mine.

On Being a Mom

The women I knew in the late fifties never thought much about having babies; we just did it. German middle-class fathers like mine shouted, "No daughter of mine will rent her own apartment after graduation!!!" and daughters like me quickly got engaged, married (four days after graduation), and became pregnant like a chain reaction. I was twenty-three and happy, doing what everyone did.

My daughter, at twenty-three, had no such knee-jerk response. Julie had plans. "Don't worry, Mom. I'll be married at twenty-eight and pregnant at thirty," she told me when she was twenty-six and we were talking about jobs, commitment, settling down.

"Do you have someone in mind?" I asked, because she hadn't mentioned anyone special lately.

"No. But I will," she smiled. When she was twenty-nine, we met Doug. A great guy; they are in love.

So what's different, you might ask. She and I both began with an idea of marriage and found a man to fulfill it. But my response was reactive, born of cowardice, my father's high blood pressure, and a savior with sexy lips. Hers came from options: to marry or not, to have kids or not. "Whatever makes you happy," Stu and I kept saying. No one was shouting.

From the day she graduated from college and started living my apartment-in-Manhattan fantasy, I envied her. Her freedom didn't depend on jumping from our house to a husband's bed with no break in between. She was young and single and could pursue whatever she wanted with whomever she wanted.

But lately I see a downside to such choice: the ante for happiness gets raised. Those who do decide to marry and have kids had better know what they are doing. We felt no such obligation. I put the kids to bed at seven because *I* had had enough (and my one book by Dr. Spock said fine). Stu played with them when he was home, for twenty minutes or an hour, depending on how *he* felt that day. No "I ought to's"—except on Sunday mornings when I slept and the work on his desk was officially off-limits until eight in the morning.

My daughter's generation expects far more of itself. They insist on being perfect parents and read scores of books on how to accomplish this. The prospect can be overwhelming, I learned from one terrific friend who, at thirty-five, didn't think she had enough patience and skill for motherhood. Her sister's kids exhausted her after an hour and they stayed up until midnight.

"How did you finally decide?" she asked as we walked along the canal near my house. I felt like a guru, dispensing revelations.

"My pregnancy test results arrived on the same day as my first job offer," I said, sheepishly, as trees in brilliant red and gold leaves hung upside down in mirrorlike water. I had no grand answer for her except that I never regretted that day. It meant emptying diaper pails and organizing play groups until, three years later, someone offered me a part-time teaching job that matched the hours my son was in nursery school, so I took it.

I have worked with increasing seriousness ever since, but it is being a mother that has amazed me the most. I wouldn't have predicted this. As a child I played with dogs more than dolls and never felt motherlike until I held my own children. (I was the baby-sitter who turned clocks ahead so the kids had to go to bed earlier.) In today's world I might well have opted against children—I'd travel around the world like my son or do fieldwork on monkeys in Kenya like my niece. I might not have gotten around to children in time, and that makes me sad.

So does the emotional juggling that today's new mothers live with daily: how much to work, how much to stay home. Our generation never struggled with this unless we were flat broke. I got out of the house by selling sweaters from six to midnight at the mall while my daughter had colic, I worked nights at the checkout counter of the library while my son teethed, and I started a community children's newspaper when my kids were old enough to become reporters, but none of that involved guilt, planning, or full-time commitment. I could still be home, whenever needed.

Stu was tenured and both kids were in junior high before I took a no-credit graduate course at Rutgers, liked it, and decided, thanks to a professor who liked my final paper, to do more. Four years later, a month before I turned forty, I received my doctorate and began a teaching career at a college two hours away. Then it was Stu, whose office is three minutes away, who came home if needed.

"All my professors will say, 'What a waste!'" one young Ph.D. in economics said to me recently. She was feeling defensive about quitting her job at the World Bank to be with her five-month-old daughter. She was looking for part-time work instead.

"I can get great daycare," she said, "but I don't want to miss out on this stage of her life." I couldn't argue with that. In my day of meager expectations, she would have needed no justification. Graduate school, training programs, what we wanted to become seemed to evolve, somehow, between carpooling and consciousness-raising groups.

Julie says that I will be a grandmother in two or three years. She and Doug have decided to stop paying two rents and get married. I wonder if, as a mother, she will put her nine-year career on hold, especially if they take on a big mortgage. I wonder if she will want me to baby-sit while she travels or works late and whether I will have the patience to play for hours again.

Our house is quiet. We have become used to a childless rhythm, so how will I manage Lego towns and Barbie dolls and Dungeons and Dragons? Fortunately, I am feeling no pressure to decide. I suspect it will just happen, like the rest of my life.

Sewing Lesson

Stu has decided to show Alan how to sew on a button. His were popping, our son told us, because of trying to cook for himself now that he's moved into his own apartment. Frozen pizza and pasta, mainly, until a girlfriend taught him how to stir-fry. So now his weight has steadied with veggies and rice, but the buttons are still off.

The two sat on the couch, their heads close together, while Stu struggled to thread a needle on the fourth try. A big hole, so easy, I thought as these dark-haired, sturdy look-alikes (one, half a head grayer and fifty pounds sturdier than the other) struggled with great intensity while I watched from the cherry rocker opposite them, resisting the urge to say, "Let me!"

My mother, her mother, my mother-in-law, and all my aunts would be ashamed of my inaction, especially my grandmother. She did everyone's buttons, hems, seams, tablecloths, and holey socks until she went blind at eighty-eight. Her carved wooden box filled with lavenders, blues, greens, reds, whites, and yellows spooled in a million shades, her army of needles stuck into satin pincushions, her hoards of neatly sorted buttons, hooks, and snaps—all were but an arm's reach away from anyone's crisis.

What my grandmother didn't do as seamstress, my mother did as knitter, making everyone sweaters, scarves, and hats in intricate patterns of softness that caressed or tickled, not like my aunt's scratchy ragg-wool creations. Those heavy, no-nonsense orange and fire-engine-red turtlenecks—"From the Needles of Tante Sophie"—were no match for my mother's pastel reindeers leaping delicately across fine-stitched cables and onto matching hats, no labels needed.

I used to help, raising my arms up like posts so my mother could wind her yarn around them, and I felt honored—until I was eight and discovered horses. Then any budding apprenticeship these three women hoped to nurture in me was ended by the thrill of galloping through Forest Park like the Lone Ranger. I always chose Sultan over sitting with Mom. The tension of holding his reins just right so he would prance high was no match for knitting or stitching limp cloth.

I did sew, under duress, in home economics at Halsey Junior High, doing backstitch and running stitch; but the class made me act silly, like Wendy and Susie in their lacy Peter Pan collars. I preferred playing kickball and spin the bottle with boys who sawed two-by-fours in wood shop across the hall. Sewing had too many little stitches—all under control.

I did knit Stu two-thirds of a green ski sweater once. It was right after we married, and I, wanting to show handmade devotion, finished everything but one sleeve (my mother finished it when she visited). And I had sewn curtains for the children's rooms: big blue elephants with yellow trumpets. I liked doing curtains. They happened fast and you saw your efforts daily on the wall. Repaired buttons, hems, ripped seams—all my grandmother's strengths—went unrecognized until they fell apart again. And my mother's art took forever to knit and then stayed, mostly, in a dresser drawer. I wanted fame like Gloria Steinem's and a reputation like my dissertation advisor's, who was a keynote speaker at conferences everywhere. So along with the rest of my women's consciousness-raising group, I had a midlife garage sale and put my almost-new sewing machine on the lawn for fifteen dollars. (I had no buyers; it's still in the basement.)

I did do sewing emergencies, usually before a senior prom or when the last of Stu's shirts landed in the spare laundry basket, out of commission. Until then the other debuttoned mishaps kept piling up despite vehement harangues of "Where the hell are my shirts?"

Then one day, someone—either Stu or I—bought the Button Machine. Stu, who likes machines and had figured out the microwave and the VCR, figured out the Button Machine. This way he could sit on the edge of his side of the bed, after I already have turned off my light, and be his own button man. The high-tech, hypodermic-like needle can sew two or three buttons a minute, so never again has he had to yell or beg for a button.

Our son now has this power. I suspect our daughter, Julie, will never ask for it, preferring to take her stuff to New World Cleaners around the corner, which does buttons, ripped seams, and hemlines. With her fifteen-hour workday Julie has no time or patience for domesticity. She once invited me over for a drink and served water.

I kept on rocking while father and son worked on tying a double knot and pushing the needle through some ratty tennis shorts. I felt a camaraderie that had begun years before when, using a library book as guide, they put a new roof on a old shack so that Alan, then a sullen thirteen-year-old, could have a hideaway. It continued, sporadically, on weekends of raking leaves, cleaning out gutters, and now, sewing on buttons.

"These were pants before they became shorts," Alan announced proudly. He, like his father, is partial to what's old. Which is good because the Button Machine was at home in New Jersey and this male bonding, renewed in a New Hampshire cabin, involved sewing by hand like my grandmother did.

"Leave enough space between the button and the fabric, or the button won't go through the buttonhole," I advised, rising from the rocker to take an aerobic walk around the lake. The morning was too sunny and crisp to let it pass me by, I assured myself, leaving the two on the couch, men who take care of themselves.

Closet Fantasies

As always when the dogwood blooms pink outside our bedroom window, Stu and I "do the clothes." This involves taking plastic lawn bags full of soiled winter clothes to the cleaners so when they come back we can hang them, with mothballs, in the new cedar closet on the third floor. The cedar alone doesn't work, we discovered last fall when moths ate three of my sweaters and eight of Stu's ties, some of which were not even wool.

Stu and I do all this so that we can bring down the summer clothes that have hung optimistically all winter. Half of these items haven't been worn in ten or twenty years, but we keep thinking "maybe this year . . ." so they don't land on the giveaway piles we force ourselves to make every spring. On these piles go pants with cuffs worn away by a hipless husband whose pants keep slipping below his belly for lack of suspenders; my unbleachable blouses with indelible grease spots that are located below the pin/scarf camouflage line; bad buys that have served penance in the closet long enough; whites so yellowed by bleach that no one can begin to debate their ever looking like new again; and fabrics so thin, holey, and colorless that even though they are hard to part with, we manage. Only about four or five items per year for me, two for Stu, who keeps rescuing everything "to wear around the house."

I try to set him straight. "This should go," I say yearly, putting my fingers in the holes of his old MIT sweatshirt, ready to rip. We can always use new rags.

"Do it and *I* go!" he says, like Clint Eastwood in an ambush, and counters with my blue bellbottoms, the ones that I wore pushing the kids' stroller. "How about these? Nobody wears these anymore."

"They will," I say, grabbing them. "They're coming back."

The survivors, his and mine, get carried up and down the stairs, year in and year out, even though half of them never have the safety pins from the cleaners removed. No matter. They are vessels of hope, past and future, the way we imagine who we were and might still be—you never know—especially when they look expensively new, like my long chiffon skirt and matching shawl, last worn to my nephew's wedding, circa 1970.

I press the gay green and pink flowers against me as images of the Rainbow Room, Stu and me doing the tango, dance before me. I repeat the ritual with my blue-striped bargain knit that I bought at Loehmann's ten years ago. And the slinky red and white silk with the military shoulders and wide Velcro belt. They all go in the closet, in back, next to my hermetically sealed wedding dress.

My husband's promise lies in his Bermuda shorts, the same ones he had on in the Grand Canyon snapshot on the mantelpiece. That was thirty years ago, before his midlife spread, and the madras looks like new because he hasn't worn them since. "I still like these," Stu says every year, sucking his stomach in, and I tell him to save them. After our diet, *I'll* wear them.

After our diet. These are the key words. Because two weeks before doing the clothes, we start Weight Watchers, the Atkins Diet, the Diet Center, whatever it takes to look good without a coat on. By closet time, we are down a few pounds and anything is possible. The promises of youth, passion, old beautiful clothes, they are only ten more pounds away, twenty at the most. I am already picturing myself in my red, see-through, sixties gauze dress, as heads turn. Stu is seeing himself diving off the high board in tight Speedo trunks, unscathed. This is also the time when we linger in front of store windows, imagining new acquisitions for the new/old us: a black lace bodysuit like my daughter's, a sleek purple turtleneck for a nineties man with no tire around his waist. Yes, this is the year. Watch!

After the clothes have been rehung or placed in bags and the bed is cleared again, I go to my unbelievably neat closet where, for a few days, life is under control. I pick something to wear for hauling this winter's rejects and survivors to their fates in the Salvation Army dumpster outside of Superfresh in the shopping center parking lot. I will fondle the khakis I wore when I fell in love, the jeans I bought last June after Weight Watchers, and put on my black corduroy pants with the elastic waist . . . Now there's an item I'll never give away.

Meat Loaf in the Freezer

Today I am leaving two giant meat loaves in the freezer—hand-molded and baked by me for Stu, who will be alone in New Jersey while I'm in Aspen, Colorado, for a two-week writers workshop. The soft, round mounds topped with ketchup, mustard, and brown sugar are meant to keep my spirit powerful while I'm gone.

I would have made two quarts of fruit soup, too, but Stu said not to bother. He didn't even care if I made meat loaf. He would manage fine with the deli down the street, or else he'd get some women to cook for him now that he's a bachelor. "Joke, joke," he said when I glared. "Make the meat loaf, I love meat loaf."

He does, too, especially this recipe found in an Amish cookbook we bought once in Pennsylvania; it's filled with reassuring titles such as "Children's Favorite Meat Loaf," illustrated by eighteenth-century block prints of women with spatulas, stirring giant pots. I had not made the recipe in years, I forgot I had it, in fact, until my mother asked what I was cooking for Stu before I left. She looked grim at my going and so did Stu's mother when he announced, first thing after we walked into her apartment last week, that I was leaving him for two weeks.

"For a workshop—part of my job," I said quickly. She kept scowling (*her* meat loaves never needed freezing!) and Stu grinned. The brave son. The brave husband. Modern, liberated, uncared for, but surviving.

Because of my meat loaf. Last year, on my longest trip before this one, I had called from Dallas every night for a week and asked, "What did you do for dinner?" imagining him dining by candlelight with someone who had a nine-to-three job and cooked Julia Child's gourmet breakfasts.

"I ate meat loaf. Delicious," Stu would say, and I'd beam with love into the receiver. No matter if I were going to a French café with some friends and then to a jazz concert on the town green. I was not like the woman in my workshop, I assured him, who had tired of the man she lived with and was going reggae dancing. I was tired and was going to bed early.

"Alone, I hope," he would joke. (Ha!)

"Alone," I would laugh, flattered, and I would think about the anthropologist with the velvet voice who had invited me to see the Yucatan with him—and his three kids.

"Two weeks in the Rockies? How'd you manage that?" asked my friends, grinning, when I said I was off, not to hear papers on the composing process at the College Composition and Communication Conference, but to talk, write, and listen to poetry with people in black vests and silky shirts. I had loved this idea and glowed with possibility until my dead aunt Sophie appeared in my dream. Spatula in hand, she warned that I would come home to an empty house, my husband gone, and it would be my own damn fault. "A smart wife over forty stays home," she said, stirring her cauldron of sauerbraten. "Even under forty."

"You're wrong," I countered. "Stu is not a German husband, not like my father and Uncle Kurt. 'Sophie this, Sophie that' for fifty-three years. Stu understands. Stu likes independence."

"You'll see," she kept repeating in elegiac tones until I leaped out of bed, sweating.

She had touched the guilt nerve that had started years before when I began staying overnight at school once or twice a week to save on gas and on teaching energy. "Just sit back and relax. Have some wine," Stu would say when I walked through the doorway every Tuesday night, and sometimes on Thursdays, too late to make dinner. He and the kids would be darting around like a team, pouring drinks, setting the table, and cracking jokes about the Chinese takeout that Stu had bought on the way home from his office three blocks away.

I'd fume at my exclusion. *I* wanted to open white boxes of rice and steamed dumplings, too, not sit still on a chair while visions of Aunt Sophie and my mother-in-law sneered. Only after dinner, after *I* had done the dishes (a task I have hated since I was six), did I relax, my turf reclaimed. I was back on the team until Monday morning, when everything repeated itself, for years, until the kids grew up and left home, and we ate out. Ten years later my daughter watches *Nightly News* after work, her feet on the coffee table, while Doug shops, cooks, orders takeout, whatever he thinks they want. Newly in love, she fears no retribution—but she never knew Aunt Sophie.

"What are you doing for dinner?" I will ask Stu tomorrow night when I call from Aspen—before I meet my friend Don, from Arizona, for dinner. If Stu says, "I'll see how I feel," who can blame him? But I do. I want him eating meat loaf for fourteen nights and loving every bite.

Negotiating Monogamy

For Stu monogamy is like being on a diet: break it with one small, delicious bite and you end up eating everything in the refrigerator. Plus you're too full for dinner.

I have resisted him on this. "You sound like my orthodox grandfather," I said when we first started talking about being faithful, around five years after the honeymoon. It was the 1960s, and "open marriage" (meaning permission to sleep with whomever) was in vogue.

"That may be, but if you have an affair, I'll divorce you," Stu kept saying, never one to be fashionable.

"How could you, so easily?" I would ask, amazed that he could say good-bye just like that. We had so much going—a new house, two little kids—but I didn't doubt him, a stubborn man who saw the world in black and white, even if I preferred grays.

I would be more forgiving, I was sure—at least the first time. At least in theory. Yet whenever I felt his good chemistry with another woman, I felt betrayed. *I* could flirt, I *needed* to flirt, but he was only supposed to talk to dull, ugly women.

And if he did find someone perfect, I did not want to know about it. Just keep her in an emotional compartment somewhere, away from our life, I would advise, usually as we sat in a traffic jam, bumper-to-bumper. (Playing marital "what ifs" was the way we passed the time before books on tape took over, around year twenty.)

Of course I would know anyway, I was sure. I knew as soon as he walked through the doorway whether he would kiss my neck or complain about leaves on the driveway. I knew when he climbed into bed whether he would read for an hour or shut off the light and roll toward me. So I would know (wouldn't I?) whether or not it would be safe for him to disappear with a particular woman into the kitchen for ice cubes, and for how long.

I could never understand spouses who had no idea, like the husband in a novel I just read. His wife of twenty-seven years wrote a note and left, her handmade macramé purse still under the groceries she decided not to bring into the house before catching a bus. Melting ice cream stuck to credit cards, lipstick, keys, Tylenol—and the man was floored; he'd thought everything was fine. No wonder she left. She probably was having an affair with a neighbor just to see if her husband would notice.

That is what my friend Greta is doing. She took a lover last summer when her husband began traveling all week and has another lover for weekends, which her husband spends watching ballgames. Now she is raising the ante: stay or go? Should she continue with men who are nice but evoke no grand passion? Or should she fall sufficiently in love to say good-bye fearlessly? Or just go and see what happens? We debate her options weekly over cappuccino in the shopping center, as we did ten years earlier for me. It was when Stu was working day and night at a new job as department chair, and I was ready for sex, murder, whatever it took not to feel like his worn-out slippers, night after night.

"I'd prefer he had a mistress," I had told Greta then. "She'd take less time, and Stu's guilt might make him put down the morning newspaper." I was full of largesse until I met his new twenty-nine-year-old assistant, who was a redhead (his color of preference) and available to work late. I would imagine them spread-eagled on his couch beside a bottle of champagne. And if, when I called, there was no answer, I would dial every five minutes until he picked up.

"Oh, I was on the john."

"Oh."

I chose to believe him. After all he *was* the man with the ultimatum about affairs.

One funny thing I have noticed about jealousy: the closer I come to another man's bed, the more I imagine Stu with someone else. When I've been at Louie's Bar sharing poems (which Stu doesn't write) and talking about memoirs (which Stu doesn't read), and the conversation is hot (Stu is McLuhan cool) and the sexual vibes are strong (harder to come by when you share a nightly bed), I always charge through the door that night with dread—"What did you do today?"—as if he'd been where I wanted to be.

Not that my insight deters me. I love when someone interesting calls at midday with a proposition for lunch or a drink so I can whisper yes or no into the phone, feeling the world is mine. I am not like my mother, whose only post-marital dates were with my father. Not like my aunts or grandmother, whose only outside male affirmation came from joking with the butcher or postman. They had no excuse for "working" dates, no professional reason to travel alone the way I do. As homemakers their would-be assignations lacked a subtlety of option. The seduction game was either "put out or don't," with no middle ground to play on.

When I told Stu about Greta, he said she was a fool. Love is a 100 percent commitment, and if Greta was so miserable, she should leave Don, he said, rolling onto his stomach so my thumbs could rub up and down his spine.

"But one person can't give you everything," I countered. "If you died, I'd have three or four lovers—one for grand passion, one for listening, one with good sense, and one to make me laugh."

"Just so you wait until I'm dead," he said.

I was not intimidated after so many years, not with a job that provided health insurance. It is just that I do not know how to make my perfectly logical fantasy work. Of friends who have tried, only three have succeeded, not counting Greta, whose marriage may or may not last. But they are all people with enormous discipline, the kind who can take two bites of chocolate mousse and leave the rest. (I ask for seconds right away.) They are lovers of secrets, the ones who as kids kept hideaway forts to themselves. (I was always jumping out from behind the couch saying, "Here I am!") They probably played house happily as part of a threesome and never asked, "Who do you like better?" (My best friend was always the one who instantly answered "Mimi.")

My cousin Sammy had eight close friends, his whole baseball team; they were all the same to him and to each other as long as they hit well. He is still like that, he told me when we had Thanksgiving at his house. He loves his wife, but he also loves other women, plenty of them, and after twenty stormy years, he and his wife have worked it out: no one nearby, and don't talk about it.

"It works for them," I told Stu as we drove home, bumper-to-bumper and stuffed with turkey.

"Fine, but not for us," said Stu. I was relieved, which annoyed me, because the next day Stu was taking his freckled secretary (another redhead) out for a birthday lunch, and I had resolved to feel generous, like the Mormon wives I read about: six of them sharing one man, by their choice.

Their husband would make an appointment to visit each of them, like in the old dating system I grew up on: "Call a week ahead, please, or I'll be busy." These women liked the arrangement because they could share rent and childcare and cooked special meals only on the nights when their turn came. If the man is vigorous enough, why not, I concluded, clipping the story to show Stu. It was almost Sunday afternoon, and he was still sleeping when I climbed back into bed, curling around him to warm my icy feet. Those Mormon women couldn't be doing this, I realized, because their man would be gone by now.

I should say that I have resolved my struggle with monogamy by having several mad passionate affairs and have convinced myself that renowned lovers like Tristan and Isolde were right: Monogamy is for uninspired wimps. Or I should say that I have been as faithful as Penelope to Odysseus and embrace my virtue, once and for all.

I will not say either. Other men tempt me with regularity, thank God, making me feel good on bad days when my ego needs stroking, and Stu, deep in his own problems, doesn't notice. Without these outside reinforcements, I would feel as trapped and invisible as the turn-of-the-century wives in *Enchanted April*, available on video. The two were tight-lipped, slump-shouldered, and battered by round-the-clock spousal demands until a secret, no-husband vacation infused them, long before Betty Friedan, with boldness. They talked back to ultimatums— No dear, thank you, I will not, good-bye—with an easy smile and headed to Italy. They unpinned their hair, flirted with sexiness, and felt a generosity that comes only from playing by your own rules. They liked themselves again and, bingo, their husbands noticed.

I understand this solution—one that does not necessitate leaping into someone else's bed, just the ongoing possibility of it.

That's What You Get for Being Faithful

For twenty-eight years I've been faithful to a dimly lit grocery down the street from us, which, though it looks like a dump, stocks the best meat and local produce around. That's why I was taken aback when I was asked for my ID card. "But you know me!" I said, my pen and checkbook in hand. After all, my hair was the same color, my face was unlifted, so why the sudden mistrust? Besides I hadn't seen my card in ten years and didn't have a clue as to where it was.

"Sorry, you need a card. New store policy," said one of the ever-changing teenagers who had replaced Ruthie and Elaine when the store was remodeled into an upscale gourmet market a few months ago. These cheerful checkout women with their optimistic "So how ya' doin' today?" made shopping tolerable even on the most miserable days. I'd been told that they had retired, which surprised me since they had twice the energy I had, white-haired or not.

"Where's Frank? He'll vouch for me," I snapped. Frank, a gracious Hungarian with a tweed jacket and a curved mahogany pipe, was another reason that I have preferred this local store all these years. I knew that if I forgot my wallet and checkbook, he would wave me on as if I were a Hapsburg princess, "Do not worry, Madame." Or if I brought back milk that had soured after three days, he'd offer his old-world smile and say, "Take another, please." And then we'd talk photography, his passion. He'd advise me on 35 mm film for indoor and outdoor use or 200 v. 400 asa, just as he'd advise me on the best honeydew melons.

"Frank is off this week," said the sour teenager, who was eyeing the clock. "And anyway, the computer still needs your card."

"But I'm a regular. Don't you recognize me?" All those hours I had spent circling the block for a parking meter counted for nothing. Not to mention years of climbing over orange crates to get at the zucchini or shuffling dairy carts all around to unblock the center aisle so I could go by.

"Sorry, a man has been cashing bum checks, lady. That's the new policy." He started tapping his fingers and looking at a young blond behind me, who was tapping her Trident gum pack.

"Do I look like a man? Besides, he's just one person . . . like me."

I bridled, the boy shrugged, and he took my check. "Next time you'll need a card."

I loaded my packages into the cart, muttering about how out-dated loyalty had no chance in this state-of-the-art world. Hadn't AT&T just downsized my neighbor after thirty years of working there? Hadn't my cousin traded in her husband for a young tennis partner without spinal stenosis? I headed past the kiwi-mango stall, the sushi bar, the gourmet bread rack and out the electric doors. I should go to Shoprite, which is twice as big and spiffy, I cursed, loading packages into the trunk of my trusty Honda, with its 110,000 miles and a broken lock that can't be fixed. And I will, too, Frank or no Frank, if I can't find my ID.

Sultan and the Red Honda

Once upon a time I rode horses to be free. I'd climb on the Queens Metropolitan Avenue bus every Monday, Wednesday, and Saturday and head for Stanley's Stables twenty minutes away. There Stanley or his brother Jake would give me Sultan or Rajah or Calamity Max to ride—not around the ring like the other kids, but into Forest Park, alone.

I'd prance across Union Turnpike, even if the light were red, and gallop down trails where I'd hope picnickers and hikers would say, "Look at her go!" Up in that saddle, racing through the woods, I wasn't the shy, slouch-shouldered kid who everyone was always telling to stand up straight and smile. I was Roy Rogers, Liz Taylor, and the Lone Ranger all in one: a hero, a winner, a star.

Of course there were off days, like the time when Sultan, whom I loved best because he was wild and liked my carrots, bucked at the stable door and threw me face down into the graveled dirt. As I limped onto the bus to go home that day, blood caked at the knees of my ripped jodhpurs, everyone stared and shook their heads as if to say, "Poor girl." I didn't like that at all.

If I had my own horse, I told my dad when he took a look at me that night, this would never happen. I'd train him, so that he'd ride me even through a stable fire without shying. But my father said, "Out of the question. Horses in the city cost too much to keep. It's like renting a house."

So why don't we move out west and buy a ranch, I'd asked every day for months, thinking how I'd race across the fields, herding horses with all the cowboys, my blond hair flying (even though I was brunette). My dad kept saying, "Sorry." I had to settle for horses for hire, two dollars an hour, three days a week.

And that's what I did until guys with broad shoulders became more appealing than a rented black stallion. But the cowgirl stayed buried somewhere in me, long after I seriously wanted a horse; some unfulfilled twinge stirred when a rodeo came on *Wide World of Sports* or "Ghost Riders in the Sky" played on the radio. Once when a girl riding bareback on her palomino loped past me and my small children on a towpath near our house, I even called the local stable to see about riding again. Ring-only riding was all they had now, the owner said sadly. Insurance costs were too high for trail rentals. For that you needed your own horse.

That's why when Stu said, "Take the Dodge" as we discussed how I'd commute through hours of backwoods to my first full-time job in eighteen years, I said no. True, the car had another good fifty thousand miles in her, and the leatherette interior looked like new. True, he offered four new tires and a new muffler for a safe ride, but I wanted a different kind of car: one with a stick shift, a stereo with tape deck, and velour bucket seats that sat low on the road for sharp turns.

With my future paychecks as collateral, I bought one—not another anonymous station wagon like our others, but a two-door Honda Prelude in fire-engine red. That was 120,000 miles ago, and I still, at daybreak, climb into it like the Lone Ranger, heading off into the Jersey Pine Barrens to teach my 8:30 A.M. autobiography class.

I race down deserted roads, doing seventy in a fifty-miles-per-hour zone, and having no one to say, "Look at her go!" is fine—especially not the state police (who have seen me four times already) or the red-faced hunters who, during deer season, line the road with shotguns as if *I* were a parade.

Mostly there is no one, nothing except some deer or a lone hawk circling low in the sky; it is enough. The steady speed through thick walls of pine lulls me back into old woods of possibility. "What is" becomes "what could be" and for two hours a day, Monday, Wednesday, and Friday, I feel my blond hair flying in the open window.

Two Steps to One

Long before Sunday golf and football were on TV, my dad and I would take walks, not just to the corner for a seeded rye as I did by myself, but up and down all the sidewalks of Forest Hills up to Union Turnpike. I never looked at scenery then, didn't care if trees bloomed or if people painted their houses—not in the days when I was taking two steps to my father's one. All I cared about was keeping up with his fast pace without stepping on a crack. It was hard because if I jumped and darted around too much, my dad, in his deep German accent, would say, "You act too silly." He wanted a nice steady pace, something calm, rhythmical, the way he remembered life in Europe before the Nazis. He wanted none of the crazy stops and starts that misbehaved American kids like me did to drive parents crazy, just a left, right, left, right, left, right—with no fooling around.

But I wasn't fooling. Those cracks were dangerous. Step on a crack, break your mother's back, everyone in the schoolyard warned. You could even end up dead—not that second probably, unless a sidewalk heaved up the way it did in earthquakes in the movies, but in a week, or month, or year, maybe. You might go to sleep one night, feeling safe, and never wake up, because in your dream you fell through a crack and couldn't climb back out. And even if you called forever—Mom, Dad, help me!—they couldn't hear, so you'd be stuck underneath like my sister Hannah, who died when she was four, three years before I was born. Strep throat, they said, and that night it happened, just like that.

Of course I don't believe in cracks anymore. Nor do I worry about the ones in our walls; the painter can spackle them up when he comes again. I know the cracks in my coffee cups don't leak; we've used them all right for years. And the cracks in my face are dignified, according to Gloria Steinem. "Wear them proudly," you earned them, she said yesterday on a talk show. I try.

Stu and I are walking more. It's good for the heart, the doctor says, so I've come full circle—walking the sidewalks again. We go down to Lake Carnegie where the willows, year after year, lean over the water. We go uptown to Nassau Street, passing cars that are stuck, bumper-to-bumper, on overloaded streets. But mostly, especially now, in spring, we go to side streets of flowering dogwoods and cherry trees that make everything, even a peeling house, look good.

"Ooooh, look at that!" I say on almost every block, pleasuring in blossoms, new grass, and fresh paint that the child in me never noticed. But I still look down to stay off broken sidewalks heaved up from tree roots. And I touch an occasional crack in the seams of cement only if I have to, for keeping up a smooth gait: right, left, right, left, left, left.

My mother always walked fast, too fast for me, her high heels tapping on sidewalks as I trailed her from Best & Company to Altmann's to Orbach's, shopping for "nice outfits" for the daughter who wanted to be a cowgirl in Arizona. A pink jacket with baby doll sleeves, a dress of sweetheart roses, Mary Jane shoes, shiny and tight. They will be perfect for you, she'd say, beaming from store to store. Trust her. All I had to do was smile, uncross my arms, and stop dragging my feet. But what did she know, a mother who had come from Germany two steps ahead of the Nazis, four years before I was born in Queens? Germany had no cowgirls.

I outgrew those mother-daughter struggles, or so I thought. I wear what I want (even if it is not in Arizona), listen to my mother when it suits me, and charge through life as well as she ever did. I never became a shopper, preferring to work full time, while she takes on Bloomingdale's, volunteers in a hospital gift shop, and visits her great-grandchildren with the same single-minded determination she once gave to my wardrobe.

"The boxes on my calendar are filled!" she tells me regularly. She isn't like Mrs. Herbert next door, who stays home and feels sorry for herself because she's alone. My mother has resisted this temptation ever since my father left her alone for a month with two small children in a

42nd Street hotel the summer they arrived. He headed for Boston, looking for work, saying, "Cheer up, Geddle. We escaped, didn't we?" Half a century later, decades after he died, my father's resolve is still hers; and it is powerful—as long as she keeps busy.

Lately she has slowed down a bit; I find myself taking half steps when we walk sometimes, my arm linked to hers in case she stops the way I did long ago when my legs ached on those Saturday shopping trips. Growing pains, she used to say with certainty, pulling me off whatever bench or soft chair I had found while she patrolled new aisles of clothes for her version of me. Come on.

But last night when we crossed Second Avenue, my mother was again my old mom, minus her high heels. It was cold, we had just eaten at her favorite pasta restaurant, and her five-foot frame was out in front, chin against the wind. She was telling me why I shouldn't drive the fifty miles back to New Jersey that night: the roads were too slippery from the snow, there'd be gridlock at the Lincoln Tunnel, and God knows what. I should stay overnight with her, she urged. Then she tripped, flew forward, and landed face down on the sidewalk.

"Mom, Mom," I called above her, running after her gold-rimmed glasses, which had skidded away. "Are you all right?" Her white hair was turning red as I knelt down and turned her over. Blood poured from her nose, her forehead, and I pressed against the wound, the way I did when Julie, at three, fell against the edge of the coffee table.

My mother was crying softly, "Let me get up! I want to go home." Two, three, five people had formed a circle saying no, she needs an ambulance, call an ambulance. The gash over her eyebrow couldn't be more than an inch or two long, I saw, wiping it with a Kleenex. Puddles of blood sat on the surface of her red suede coat, waiting to be shaken off; there were no stains. Someone brought a blanket, I put her plaid scarf under her head, still pressing hard against the blood. The nosebleed slowed, the forehead was just oozing.

"Mimi, please, take me home. I'm fine," she whimpered, and the child in me trusted her. If my mother said she was fine, she was fine—even if the gray-haired man in the camel coat had just taken out his cell phone to dial 911, and the young woman who brought the blanket from nowhere had raced to the corner to get the police. I didn't say to do that.

"Can you sit up?" I asked, thinking it's only two blocks to her apartment house. We could walk or take a cab and then call her doctor from home as she wanted. I pulled her up a few inches; she was woozy, and then I saw a huge blot of red on the back of her head. How could that happen? A hole has gone through her, I decided, even as I kept replaying the image of her forehead hitting a perfectly smooth pavement.

The sirens came closer. The ambulance lights flickered across faces; the gray-haired man turned a half-second of yellow, a delivery boy shimmered in blue, but my mother, below the spin of lights, remained streaked with red.

"You *have* to go to the emergency room," I said, without a hint of doubt. I was now one of the circle that surrounded her. She would have no choice, she knew from my tone, and shut her eyes. "Mother, don't go to sleep, keep talking, stay awake." I sounded as I had when my children fell off bikes and beds with regularity, and I was the adult on duty, twenty-four hours a day.

Two men in tan uniforms lifted her onto the stretcher as I stroked her hand—Mom, Mom. She looked so small and frail. Her eyes were turning black and blue, her nose was swelling to twice its size. Was this my mother who had convinced me that she would keep me safe in spite of myself? I wanted *her* standing over *me*, smiling the way she used to every morning when she burst into my room—Wake up! Rise and shine!—while I pulled a pillow over my head, waiting for her maddening invincibility to go away.

"Mimi, you should wear a hat in this weather," my mother whispered, brushing the bangs off my face while they hoisted her toward the van's double doors to take her away. "Take my scarf, at least—and here's my handbag. Keep it with yours," she said before disappearing inside. I put them both over one shoulder and climbed in behind.

Weighing In between Rubens
and Modigliani

Today at the museum, I was standing in the seventeenth-century room before two giant paintings of Rubens nudes lounging, naked and un-assuming, in meadows and on bath rims, dimples on their butts, rolls between breasts and bellies that double by leaning over. They don't care. Weight Watchers, the cover of *Vogue*, cellulite fear have not de-fined these fleshy goddesses of Grace and Pleasure. They see them-selves as beautiful, and within their gilded frames, I believed them totally. I wanted to climb in, strip, and forget about holding my breath so my stomach stays flat.

But through the archway were the Modiglianis: slim, angled, solemn, and sophisticated. They know how to pose, these long-necked beau-ties with tipped heads and sloping shoulders, expecting admiration. They are women who never bothered with over-blouses or elastic waist-bands, who could eat five mince tarts at the office Christmas party if they wanted. But they never do. It's always the Rubens women with the double chins doing that; the Modiglianis are over by the crudités.

I am the one—five feet three inches and age fifty plus—who is in between, helping myself to home-baked tarts, which are my favorite, and to carrots, which make me feel that I can get away with two tiny tarts. So I am always ten pounds more than I'd like to be. Never fif-teen more because that shocks me into action: eating cottage cheese and Kavli crackers and stepping on the scale five times a day. And never just right because thin seems dangerous. Once more I am the child set against white pillows, whose worried parents hover holding a spoon of Jell-O at her lips—Eat! Eat! (or you'll die).

I worry when others get thin, too. When my daughter went from a size ten to a size two, she was delighted that at last she looked like her friend Nora, whose body never betrayed its androgynous grace. I was beside myself. I liked hugging a soft, pliable body. Suddenly I felt bones, the way I did with my cousin Dora, who vowed, six months from being fifty, to weigh what she did at twenty-two. Her round face became lean, her curves angled, but instead of growing regally sleek like a Modigliani, she seemed smaller, less significant, like anonymous women I see on buses.

I have started to slouch when I'm around her, the way I did in fifth grade when, overnight, I grew breasts and hips, and my best friend Arlene stayed flat as a boy. All year I wore giant men's shirts, except when I wore tight angora sweaters. The boys still loved Arlene's blond curls, but my body was their adventure. Richie Pear put thumbtacks on my bus seat to flirt, John Vinocur pulled me into the closet at parties, even though Arlene, with her triple-A training bra, was the one they protected walking home.

There is a photo taken of me in high school. I am half-kneeling on my front lawn, buxom and freckled, my auburn hair in the prescribed pageboy of Forest Hills girls of the fifties. When I see that tight, white sweater and red plaid Bermuda shorts, I say to myself: "Wow, you were slim!" I keep expecting to see the rolls that had disappeared two years earlier, when I gave up hot fudge sundaes for a date with the best kisser in the Midway Theater balcony. Next to me is a five-foot-nine-inch redhead named Paula, who was my new best friend. If she had looked like my daughter's friend, I, too, might have dropped to a size two, but Paula towered over me; her dress size was two sizes larger than mine, and half the guys were too short for her. A perfect best friend. We would stand at Penn Drug on Friday nights, flirting with everyone after the basketball game, and my curves felt charmingly sexy—hips, breasts, and all.

I fell in love to get more of that feeling: no boys with slim hips and little behinds for me. I wanted 180 pounds of broad chest and shoulder who had a busty mother. She was framed in gilt over his blue couch, lying on Jones Beach like an odalisque, surrounded by great-looking guys who couldn't get enough of her. Her son had to be right for me, I decided on that couch, feeling beautiful in his arms.

In 1957 the word still had variation. *Beautiful* could mean full-bodied and seductive like Kim Novak or slim like June Allyson, with her tiny wrists and cinch-belted wide shirts. I would imitate one or the other, depending on how much I ate and who was on the movie marquee that week. I never felt cheerleader-slim like my older sister, who loved guys of all sizes, who always loved her in return. But I felt competitively curvy until Jackie Kennedy hit the White House and beauty became defined as skinny in a pillbox hat. The abundance of Marilyn Monroe, Lana Turner, and Kim Novak gave way to the minimalism of Audrey Hepburn and Twiggy, and every girl I knew adopted the same pipe dream: to become a size two.

I am revising that dream thirty years later, not because of realism—Is that ever a consideration when weight is concerned?—but because of observations made in the women's locker room. Slim women look good in clothes but not in the raw, I have noticed since I began swimming three days a week to stay in shape. I am amazed by the transformations: women in elegant power suits become nondescript when naked, as if style and allure depend on camouflage and deprivation. Bony shoulders, protruding rib cages, pencil-like thighs. These images depress, even frighten, me, as they did long ago when I was a child watching the *Movie News* stories of World War II survivors.

It is the huge Rubenesque woman, eight months pregnant and falling out of her 38d bra and too-tight sweatpants, who seems like a goddess. When she is undressing, three lockers down from mine, I remember suckling my baby daughter, my belly still swollen, my breasts overflowing, while I, for the first and maybe only time, felt beautifully huge, opulent, generous. But the woman dresses quickly, as do I.

When my mother took a bath, I often sat on the rim of the tub, telling of my P.S.3 adventures while she half-floated on her back, looking fine. But as soon as she stood up, one foot over the side, her unplanned rolls and stretch marks unnerved me until they disappeared into girdle and bra. And the scar from a gallbladder surgery puckered like a bad hem across her belly; I wanted it fixed.

Once dressed my mother was not fat, not like half of my German aunts, uncles, and cousins who sat around every Sunday, bulging from too much bratwurst and *kartoffelsalat*. They had better watch out, the other half of the aunts, uncles, and cousins warned, as the family engaged in their favorite double pastime: eating while assessing who was too fat and too thin. Cousin Bobby could break a chair; give him only a sliver of cake. Cousin Anna eats like a rabbit; give her two slices. My sister could eat what she wanted, but she should study more. Only I was an enigma: too skinny until I was ten, too fat until I was fourteen, and then right on the edge, a figure to be watched at every meal.

40

Forty years later I lie in the tub like my mother, steaming nightly in comfort. But I get out quickly because in the mirror it is my mother I see, especially in the sagging belly that juts out without subtlety. I should do sit-ups like my daughter, but I resist, wanting to be like the German women we saw at a crowded pool in Barcelona last summer. They lounged topless in G-string bikinis, coating themselves with sun oil and drinking beer, as if there was no one to see every roll, tuck, and crease glistening in the sun. Only models like Twiggy would be that unabashed in America.

Germaine Greer, whose book on menopause sits on my night table, would urge me to go ahead, be a Barcelona woman, because if you are over fifty, men don't care anyway. And even if they do, forget *their* image of beauty and define your own, I told myself as I tried on ski pants after the museum. They refused to close, and the old me would have called Weight Watchers immediately. The new me decided I could ski in my jeans—and went to the kitchen to eat a bagel with half the dough torn out.

To eat it all would mean resigning myself to a life in caftans, like Rhona, who swoops into a room in swirling purples that forgive her bulk. I'm not ready for that—even with the new mirror I bought at the Golden Lion, the antique consignment shop in town. Stu mounted the mirror in the attic guest room, and there was the woman I wanted to be: long-necked, long-waisted, a Modigliani but with curves. All week I've been climbing the stairs to see myself in her, trying on whatever makes me want to dance all day in the angled morning light.

The Power of the Cap

I used to drive defensively on the back roads to work. In rural South Jersey, with its pickup trucks and long-finned Cadillacs, if you are a woman who overtakes, tailgates, or flicks her brights on and off too often, you can get the finger. Or an angry male might speed up, so you can't pass in time to avoid an oncoming car without braking hard in retreat—or heading for the graveled shoulder.

But that is old history. I drive the way I please and no one bothers me—because of my caboose cap. That's what is written above the tiny, red caboose on the brim of my gray-striped railroad cap that I bought from a cart at Penn Station in New York City. In it I become someone who stokes hot engines in a passing world.

It had been lying on the car floor, waiting for one of my sudden solitary walks, when my brand-new Honda's sun visor broke off for the third time. I put the cap on to shield my eyes from the glare and bingo!— the sun disappeared, much better than with sunglasses. But, oh, what other perks this cap has had! No more middle fingers and no high-speed bullying of a freckle-faced, reddish-haired, middle-aged woman who was supposed to make men feel macho on the open road. Now they don't know what to expect. They see a driver (a woman?) with a crazy cap and a set jaw, staring straight ahead, and I hear their minds clicking. Maybe she, or he, is a cop—or a nut with a .45. They behave themselves.

One day I was driving nearer home, capless, and a guy stopped short on a busy road to let someone enter from a driveway. I nearly rear-ended him, and a white van nearly rear-ended me, so I threw up my hands in disgust, which he saw in his mirror. He raised his middle finger, and I reached for my cap. I saw his eyes widen in that same mirror. He fiddled with his radio; he slumped an inch lower; he turned at the next corner. I don't think he lived on that block.

Another time I took a wrong turn off the New Jersey Turnpike and landed at an endless block of abandoned buildings lined with huge parked trucks. I slumped down, afraid to ask anyone I could find for directions—until I remembered my cap. I donned it, tipping it slightly upward above dark sunglasses, opened my window, and hailed the first guy I saw: "Hey, where's Exit 13a?"

"Go left two lights, then right," he yelled, "then left again at the fork." He had on a red cap turned backward, with a black strap like a clothesline across his forehead. Punk or good guy? Only a smile would tell, and his was broad as he pointed toward a blinking light in the distance. Five minutes later I was asking again, this time of two guys having a smoke on a loading dock.

"Which way to the turnpike?" I called, cocky as a truck driver. My voice was lost in the rev of a diesel engine. "Which way? The turnpike?" No response. No one else was around, so I had to get out, cross the street, get close. Not a problem when you're in a caboose cap and a loden green cape that looks like an army tent on the move. They stood up quickly, snuffed out their cigarettes, and sent me two blocks right and one left. Within minutes I was on the turnpike, flying along with my cap back on the floor because it was a cloudy day and I liked how the breeze let my hair fly wild.

Yesterday Stu and I were driving north to North Hampshire, into the sun. He, the engineering professor, had on his blue cap with a straight brim and chewed a toothpick as if he were a New England woodsman. I had on an impish straw hat, imagining myself as Huck Finn, who was floating down the river on the audiotape that I'd taken out of the library. I was easy, open to adventure, when a double-hitched Seltzer truck passed on my right. A muscular, curly-haired driver, cute, was looking down at my skirt that was hiked high on my thighs. A dragon climbed the inside of his arm, which was resting on his open window above me. He winked, honked, and sped up, heading for the middle lane. He raised his fist, which turned into a V for victory. My husband honked. He would not be cut off. A battle was brewing—would-be woodsman vs. dragon man—and I reached for my caboose cap, just in case.

How We Mourn the Powerful

She was dressed in a white shroud, as she had wanted, but the casket was a fine mahogany, not the plain pine of her instructions. And instead of a simple graveside ceremony—Charlie, no fuss, please!—there was a full chapel service for Rose Schwartz, with piped organ music and huge urns of white and yellow flowers.

Stu was uncomfortable. He and his brother, Howie, were used to following *her* orders. They adored their father, who adored them, but it was their mother who sat at the kitchen table year after year, listening, advising, threatening, nudging, while Charlie went down for a smoke. No cigars in her house was an ironclad rule. And Charlie listened, as he did to pretty much everything his wife had said, until yesterday when, in tears, he told his hefty, square-jawed sons—images of his Rosie—that he would honor her *his* way. She deserved the best.

"It's not really *her* decision," my sister-in-law whispered as we shivered in the November rain. The cold had come suddenly, after three weeks of Indian summer, brilliant in color. No one had expected a forty-degree drop in temperature in one day. "These events are for the living to deal with grief, not for the dead. Charlie should do whatever makes him feel good."

The rabbi, a man in a wrinkled brown suit, someone's cousin, chanted prayers as we huddled at the grave site, maybe thirty of us against the driving storm. I moved closer to Stu, who had the umbrella, and I looked for my children, wishing them close. They were off to one side, near Bobby Becky's grave—that was Rose's mother—their arms interlocked, their eyes to the ground. It was their first funeral; they were too young when my father died, and we hadn't wanted to scare them.

"Oh, my Rosie, my Rosie," Charlie wailed as he threw the first shovels of dirt into the open grave. Everyone was lined up to follow, and I squeezed Stu's hand, unnerved, for the men I grew up around never cried. "You have to be a toughie!" my dad would say, making a fist, his steel-blue eyes mocking, whenever anyone became too emotional. That's how he, like Moses, led the family out of Germany: survival meant no tears, and crying meant being a schlemiel, a softie who would never make it in this world. My grandmother was labeled a schlemiel, and I had her hazel eyes, so I had to be extra vigilant or I'd hear, "Just like Omi!" (She lived until ninety-nine.)

I watched Stu, solemn-faced, take his turn with the shovel, praying he'd be like my dad, not his. His whole body trembled facing the grave, and I thought he would buckle into the wet grass, leaving me alone. When our shoulders touched again, the shiver of Death ran through him to me, and I was afraid to lean against him.

Then it was my turn with the shovel, and I went up, the mud sticking to metal, pulling my arms toward the casket. Good-bye, I whispered to a strong, generous woman who always had an opinion as to whether we should take the job, buy the house, move—but pronounced whatever we decided "perfect," her voice booming with pride for her first-born, her *tatela*. Stu could do no wrong. I stuck the shovel back in the dirt, and Julie, my firstborn, was waiting to take it, the tears streaming down her face. I wanted to wrap myself around her. What if I died, leaving her?

Ve yiska dall, vi yiska dash. They chanted the prayer for the dead as they had for my father, and Stu began to sob in great heaves. Now he was like me, without the parent he depended on. What would he do? I put my arm around the shoulders I depended on. "It's okay, it's okay," I whispered, rubbing his back and imagining my father looking down with fist raised: "Don't be a schlemiel!" At his funeral I had controlled my tears—we all had, imagining that fist. Only afterward, in Stu's arms, did the fist fade into Stu's caresses—Don't leave me, Don't leave me— and I became the child I was afraid to be, the one who bawled at bad haircuts and sad movies and would need rescuing her whole life.

Charlie wept unabashedly as he greeted his old friends from Rodney Street in Brooklyn, where he and Rose had rented their first apartment. We were back in Queens, where they'd lived for years in a three-room flat with picture windows now covered by heavy shades. Food platters we'd ordered from Lenny's Deli were set on the credenza—corned beef, salami, slaw, rye, two mustards, baby Danish, and coffee—all arranged below a long wall of photographs.

"I talk to these pictures every day," Rose used to tell everyone who glanced at her gallery of framed children and grandchildren, performing wondrous feats. Alan, at six, rubbing noses with our dog, Karma. Chubby little Howie on a pony while Rose, radiant in a 1940s upsweep, stood on one side holding his waist and chubby big brother Stu, calm and smiling, held the reins. (Food equaled love to Rose, and fat cheeks meant success on a rug salesman's salary.) Both sons in college graduation gowns (her crowning achievement). Howie's sons laughing, half-buried in a leaf pile. Julie, on a ferry in Greece. Our wedding portrait. Howie's. And centered among us, in its gold-leaf frame, was Rose as a sexy blond on Jones Beach surrounded by four admiring boys, one of whom was a dark, handsome lad with adoring eyes. That was Charlie.

Charlie broke down again when Moe, his boyhood friend, came, and again when in walked the Moskins, who had rented the cabin in the country, next to theirs. They were all in their seventies and eighties, with canes and no cars. They had taken the A train or E train from every borough to get here in spite of the bitter cold and wind that had torn through the city's streets until every tree was colorless and bare.

All day and night visitors kept coming. Lucio, the doorman, told us how Rose had made him a dozen blintzes when his mother died. "And what a knitter she was," said Scottie, who ran the garage. "My granddaughter still wears that red sweater of hers." Harriet, who knew Rose from her bookkeeping days in Brooklyn, came from Long Island. "Every Monday night, we spoke." She broke down. "Rose gave me such good advice. How I'll miss that woman." She collapsed onto Charlie, who hugged her and everyone else who talked about his Rosie.

But he did not fall apart as Rose had predicted, maybe hoped for, when the walls of their apartment had begun to close in. She'd been housebound with emphysema for several years, leaning on the sink to cook or wash dishes, and the last year she was bedridden, breathing oxygen from a whirring tank. She'd still managed to tell Charlie exactly what to wear, where to put his shoes in the closet, what coffee cup to drink from, but it was with the fury of the sick for the healthy. "The man is hopeless. He won't survive a day without me. He can't even boil water right!" she snapped, trying to catch her breath. "The widows will be up here in a flash."

She knew what a handsome specimen this barrel-chested, full-head-of-hair man was for eighty-one, and she knew her competitors. Mrs. Atkin in 10G, who drove him to Stark's Deli for barbecued chicken every Friday. Bella, the widow in 6R, who visited daily with bags of roasted cashews. They sensed what Rose had: a true lover of women, a man happy to give, listen, and hold without taking over. Even I, over thirty years younger, liked to curl into his bear hug that was never suffocating, a cozy place to rest for awhile.

He disappeared into the bedroom, and we could hear the wailing—"Rosie, oh, my Rosie"—but before anyone could follow he reappeared, carrying her painted, pink jewelry box. "Wear this for her, will you, sweetheart?" He pressed a pinkie ring of tiny sapphires into Julie's hand. He gave me Rose's jade brooch—"She bought it for your wedding!"—and gave my sister-in-law Rose's silver choker. And to Alan he gave Rose's favorite drop-pearl earrings—"Save this for your wife, when you find her!"—and shook with tears. "If only Grandma could have met her."

We all broke down. Who could not? But I was less scared than before because Charlie, with all his tears, had one antenna raised to the real world. He asked Stu if he'd remembered to give the undertaker Rose's teeth. He asked if I could make more coffee, and he listened attentively to his sons' pleas for him to come home with them. No, he would stay here, Charlie said, refilling the milk pitcher. He had to do what he thought best.

During the next few weeks Charlie cried unabashedly each time we spoke, but he didn't keel over, he kept food in his refrigerator, he walked to the corner daily for milk and the newspaper, and he wore clean shirts. In the three years he'd watched the woman he loved drop from 160 to 70 pounds, he found within him, somehow, a power that grew with each dish he washed, each trip he made to the bank to cash a CD for her care, and now he carried on, tears and all.

A month or so later Charlie found the carrot-red and lemon rugs in the closet. They were runners that he'd bought when he worked in Macy's rug department. "Real bargains, good stuff!" he had said, sticking his finger into the nap. Rose, who made him retire a year short of his fifty-year award dinner—He's forgetful, he needs to take it easy—had put the rugs in the closet. "Too thin, too bright, too slippery!" she had scolded in front of us. Now he spread them out across the living room for visitors to step on when they came to pay their respects. And he smiled, saying, "Watch your step!" as he welcomed us in.

Towpath Therapy

Where mules, for a century, towed barges of coal for twelve-hour days from Kingston to Blackwell's Mills, Stu and I now do an hour's fast walk, past the old water locks, ancient blackwater birches, and twisted sycamores leaning over the canal like drunken sentries.

We get our rhythms right on this straight, flat trail, still called the towpath (though the last mule was here in 1932). There is no need to talk and no need not to, so words come not as snippets—Did *you* buy milk? No. Did *you* call the plumber? I thought *you* did—but as smoother, more rounded probes into vulnerability and compromise.

"Do you think we've passed our prime in tennis?" I say.

"Our bodies, maybe, but not our souls," Stu says cheerfully. "Not with as many deuces as we had."

It is the day after we lost a tennis match to a couple we used to beat, and here on the Delaware Raritan Canal, going a steady 3 mph, we are joking. But on the tennis court yesterday, all we said from game three on was: Stupid. Jerk. Move, for God sake. Get lost. And finally: That's it! Get another partner from now on.

After that, silence—until I handed him a banana this morning ("thanks") and he handed me the metro section of the *New York Times* ("thanks"). Now we are back to full sentences.

"Oh, if I were twenty pounds lighter, I'd dance like a butterfly and sting like a bee," says Stu, doing a two-step but keeping up with our rhythm. "Remember Mohammed Ali saying that?"

"You *would* move faster," I agree. His midlife tire has been growing, a touchy subject all year. "Maybe you could go to a nutrition doctor? Pam knows one and . . ."

"I'm not going to any nutrition doctor." Silence. We pass a dozen trees. "You just cook low-fat."

"I do. But you snitch peanut butter at night. The jar is half-empty already, and don't blame Alan. He's in China."

"No more. You just watch."

A woodpecker taps somewhere to the right and, to the left, eighteenth-century homes with names like Stepping Stone and Buttonwood look down, unchanged, from safe hillsides. "I'll be Jimmy Connors next year!" Another two-step. "And then you'll have no excuse"—he gives my ribs a jab—"for *not* stepping into the ball!" I laugh instead of snarl, thinking I'll sign up for Nautilus just in case. And then we look for a sturdy tree to touch and kiss under, our ritual before turning around for home.

When time is short we walk in our neighborhood, but seeing houses up close makes us talk about reseeding the lawn or calling the tree man. And there are traffic lights to stop for and cars to watch for as we step off curbs. With a ten-minute drive up Route 27 and a walk through an underpass of psychedelic metal tubing—Eureka! No more should do's, no sudden stops and starts, just a steady towpath beat—and an eye for hidden tree roots and a little horse manure. We nod to the occasional fisherman casting for catfish. We watch a canoe cutting the glassy canal surface, see two turtles sunning themselves on logs, a mallard family taking an afternoon float, and we feel no demands in this world of small surprises—except when a jogger calls out "on the right" or "on the left."

Lately I've been coming to the towpath with friends, too. It's replacing cappuccino at Rosa's Café, our new coffeehouse in town. On the towpath our heart ejection fractions improve without temptation from white chocolate brownies that aren't worth the calories. Conversations cover the usual aches and pains, kids, bosses, who's in the hospital, who's getting a divorce—but side by side on the trail, at a good clip, talk feels different.

"My niece is getting married and wants to change her name. I really gave it to her," says Pam, who is ten years younger than I am and on her third husband and fourth name. We are flying along.

"I don't know . . . Having the same name is easier with kids," I say.

"Don't be so old-fashioned. The kids can take his name. You, at least, keep an identity."

"But I was glad to give up Loewengart, which no one ever spelled right. Now if I had married Paul Kristoforski, maybe . . ."

"Who's Paul? I thought you and Stu met in high school?"

The sun is hot because we are on the part of the trail that circles Lake Carnegie, and the shade has disappeared as we cover my reminiscences of how I met Stu in bio lab by breaking his pen (which he made me pay for), and where Paul the poet fit in. And I feel the old teenage me pushing through, saying, "Walk faster, lady, keep up with her."

We move on to Pam's new pleasure—when her husband is away, she eats clam chowder at midnight. "He hates clam chowder so it's like having an affair with myself," she says. Her chest is out, she is rosy-cheeked and beaming, and I am delighted that my hip doesn't hurt. The Advil worked. I imagine Smokestack Gallagher, the infamous, champagne-drinking barge man whose picture hangs in the towpath museum, toasting us with muscles bulging. I imagine the armada of private yachts (also in the museum) saluting us on their way to winter in Florida while captains in crisp white uniforms shout, "How about coming along?" as we wave, hips swinging at a fast 4 mph, or more.

I bring my mother to the towpath when she visits from Manhattan, where walking means hard cement even in Easy Walk shoes. We take small, measured steps as she tells me about her friend dying of cancer and how much she misses my father. Life as a widow still hurts after all these years, she says, her voice cracking as I take her arm. There are so many stones on this dirt trail.

"Did you know, in Stuttgart my father bought me a wonderful red bicycle?" Her steps begin to widen. "And my brother, Walter, rode me on the handlebars—and that's how I got this!" She points to her crooked nose, which I thought she was born with. "And Dr. Nathan, remember him from Forest Hills? He said I could have plastic surgery, but I wouldn't dream of it. I am who I am," she says, laughing.

Her shoulders have straightened, wisps of now all-white hair blow in the breeze, and I let go of her arm, thinking she's all right, my mother of eighty-three. A blue heron surprises us around a bend, and we both laugh.

Today I came to walk the towpath alone. Stu is in Boston, and everyone else is tied up, so I converse with myself, running scripts of glory and disaster through my head as my feet set their own pace. What if his plane crashes? What if I didn't unplug the coffeepot? What if the curly-haired jogger in the red sweats asks me for a drink? Two young lovers are kissing in a red canoe, and I think of them tipping over, their bodies wet and clinging. Who could rescue them? Would it be me? And who would rescue me?

I walk farther than I planned to in this world where Time seems to stand still, and when I turn, the sky has darkened. A rumble comes up, still far away, but I sprint, my heart beating fast, waiting for lightning that doesn't come. Instead, a purple sunset fills the treetops and the sun squints low on the horizon as I slow to a walk, "One, two, three, four, left my wife on the kitchen floor." Giant raindrops fall and I don't miss a beat, thinking that tomorrow Stu will be home and we'll be back here together. And if he were delayed or . . . could never come again, I vow, as my shadow lengthens into dusk, I'd still come here.

Part 2: Morning Legacies

A Night for Haroset

I am not religious, I don't love ritual, so I never thought I'd be peeling apples for a Passover Seder so soon after a mastectomy. But I am. Eight days ago I was lying in Presbyterian Hospital being prepped for the removal of my left breast, and tonight I'll be dining on fine china, unused in two years, as part of a ceremony I don't have time for when I'm teaching—unless it falls on the weekend.

Julie is taking the noon train home from New York to help me. She told her boss at WQXJ that she was leaving early, which surprised me given the pressure there, Jewish holiday or no. I'm glad she did, because my mother, who makes brisket and matzo balls, is in Florida with shingles, so everything is up to us—and Weinstein's Deli. They are supplying the brisket, the matzo balls, chopped liver, and carrot kugel. I'm doing the Seder plate: arranging a platter with matzo, shank bone, parsley, roasted egg, saltwater, and horseradish for the bitterness of life; and chopping apples, nuts, honey, and wine for *haroset,* the sweetness of life. I am making a big bowl of it, even if my stitches pull.

Stu is in his study, preparing the service. Something short, I told him, twenty minutes at most, because he shouldn't get too tired—although he won't admit that. He, like me, can't believe what has happened. Two months ago we were standing on Big Burn Mountain in Colorado, surrounded by blue skies, mountain peaks, and two inches of fresh powder (the photo leans against the kitchen radio), and now I'm waiting for a final pathology report and Stu is waiting to see if his angioplasty worked. That's right. He had a heart attack two days after they found my lump, almost died, and came home from the hospital two days before I went in.

My uncles Sol, Max, and Julius still wouldn't approve of an abridged service of the Hagaddah, which means "to tell the story." All through my childhood, no lines were skipped as they sang and chanted for hours, their bald heads bent and gleaming under tiny black *kippot,* while I, the youngest child by years, sat with eyes closing from too much wine, asking how much longer. Four cups of wine for God's four promises; parsley dipped, not once but twice, in salt water for tears; bitter horse-radish, eaten with *haroset;* matzo broken, then hidden to be found; the Four Questions that I, as the youngest, had to ask so others could an-swer, explaining why this night is different from all other nights. They chanted about bondage in Egypt, firstborns saved by God, the Red Sea opening, the wandering in the desert, the Commandments, the free-dom, and still the bitterness, three thousand years of it, mixed with some honeyed apples.

My uncles are all dead, and Stu, whose family comes from Russia and Romania, does not know the German melodies I keep wanting to hear tonight, especially the one about a baby goat—*Ha Gadya, Ha Gadya*—sung triumphantly up and down the scale. And then we'd go home.

I have taken the Rosenthal dishes out of the sideboard—When *was* the last time? Thanksgiving two years ago?—and also my grandmother's crystal glasses that have to be washed by hand.

"At least buy paper plates and cups," my sister Ruth had said when she heard what I was doing. She wanted us to come to her, but I said no. I wanted to be home, just the four of us: Stu, me, Julie, and Alan. (Alan just called from his dorm to say he has one more midterm exam, in economics, and he'll be on his way.)

"If it's just you four, no one will care what you serve on," my sister had scolded. She may be right, but I want every heirloom present, so whoever is up there will see us as solid types, not flaky, and will agree that we should be around a lot longer, cancer and heart attack notwith-standing.

The sun feels good through the window as I watch Julie, her blond hair cascading around her, poke flower stems into Styrofoam for our centerpiece: red and white carnations she bought at the train station. Such a capable young woman, I found out last week when I was in the hospital. She did my nails, using the bedpan for water, brushed my hair, touched me despite the bandages. Youth, optimism, they push you on. "C'mon, Mom, you can do it!" she'd say daily, forcing me out of bed and into the halls, walking, walking, even as I tilted to the left. All that coaching I gave her and Alan—Don't be afraid of the dark, there's nothing there!—has paid off. She takes down Stu's grandmother's brass candlesticks and finds my fancy serving bowls, as if nothing has changed.

"I hope Weinstein's doesn't put chicken fat in the matzo balls. That stuff is poison for Dad now," I say, getting up from my chair to wash parsley.

"One or two won't hurt." Julie motions me to sit, like the producer she is. Six days a week she's up at four in the morning, telling sound engineers and traffic reporters and the weatherwoman when to fade in and out of the morning show.

"Well, according to Aunt Elsa, who called before seven, I should serve boiled potatoes and not ask for trouble."

Julie giggles, knowing how I feel about the family network of advice, delivered by telephone before 8 A.M. on everything from husbands to matzo balls. Matzo balls are particularly dangerous, according to family folklore, because a few too many put my grandfather in the emergency room. This warning used to be announced over the hot soup tureen just as Tante Elsa or Tante Louisa served. Now, too old to cook or travel, both of them call the warning in.

"Isn't Aunt Elsa the one who used to make that mound of honeyed nuts and cherries?" Julie asks, starting on the parsley.

"No, that's Tante Louisa—on another holiday." I can't remember the name of the cake. "She also called. Same advice."

We laugh like girlfriends, maybe because for once I offer no advice on exercise, AIDS, sunblock, and eating enough fruit. I feel happy just sitting with her, until I think of those dumplings, heavy, German, and delicious. I wish someone could make them.

The curtains are drawn, two candles flicker over the white tablecloth, damask shimmering as we gather, warm and safe, with glasses raised. *Baruch ata Adonai. Elohenu melach ha olim* . . . Stu is saying words to thank God "for redeeming us and our fathers from Egypt, and enabling us to reach this night . . ." Yes, I'll go along with that—especially since Stu is a firstborn, passed over. He could have died the morning we were getting dressed to drive me to the breast surgeon in New York. Stu's face was so gray, sweating, and then the ambulance, the IV, nitro, and the emergency room saving him with TPA, a new drug that had just arrived that morning. I'll drink to that. Amen.

Alan is following along in the text, Julie is sipping wine, and I am thinking how, like her, I never wanted to learn Hebrew as a child. We never pushed her the way my father tried to push me, signing me up for Sunday school without success. "You teach me," I'd say, reminding him how, in his village, he had to learn Torah every afternoon as a boy. He was an expert.

"Okay, I will!" he'd say, and I knew I was saved. He liked Sunday golf too much.

> May the Merciful One be blessed in the heavens and the earth.
> May the Merciful One be praised for generations without end.
> And may He be glorified in us for aeons and aeons.

Even in good years I hate all that flattery, as if this were a just world. Thank you, thank you, thank you "to the King of kings, the Holy One, blessed is He who doest good to all." In Hebrew it sounds fine, but when I read the English, I balk. What about the Holocaust, and the children in Somalia, and Mai Lai? My scar throbs. And what about me, us? We're good people, even if on high holy days I go with Stu to synagogue only because I like hearing the melodies, touching shoulders—and I don't want him to go alone.

I stop trying to follow and pour myself more wine, half-looking for scowling uncles to stop me, the way they had when my cousins kept filling my glass with sweet red Manischevitz until I giggled out of control. Alan, as the youngest, begins: *Ma nish tahna, ha layla ha zeh meekol ha laylos?* (Why is this night different from all other nights?) He sings the Four Questions in full throttle, his voice rich and confident, as if being his father's baby-sitter while I was having a mastectomy had never happened. How scared he had looked then, this young man singing like James Taylor doing "Fire and Rain." My father would have liked this rendition. Even my uncles would be pleased with such gusto about why on this night we eat matzo, the unleavened bread; taste bitter herbs; and recline, not sit, to tell the story of the Jews. (It's a long story.)

Julie is singing "Eliayhu Hanavi," her voice soft and ethereal from singing Handel's Hallelujah Chorus through four years of high school choir. She is inviting Elijah, Prophet of Cheer and Comfort, to come to us. We have set the table for him. An empty chair, a place setting, a glass of red wine poured and ready. "In his name we open the door," she reads in English, "and welcome anyone to share our Seder meal." Then she goes to the front door, and I feel an immediate draft. I hope Mrs. Nolner's cat doesn't come in like the last time Julie did this; he was hard to catch.

The outside air makes me shiver, but it passes, and suddenly I feel less abandoned. My uncles, my father, Tante Elsa and Tante Louisa, my mother, sister, mother-in-law, and everyone else who ever sat at a Passover table with me are here after all. I hear their melodies of prayer and feel their legacy of good wishes that we are here tonight, passed over. Some knot in me unties. Even if the cancer spreads and Stu slumps to the floor tomorrow, we are saying words that have been handed down for three thousand years, and they will be repeated next year, no matter what. I picture the full, rich table—Julie, Alan, whoever is left—singing *Ha Gadya, Ha Gadya.* I almost hear the right tune.

Yes, yes, okay, I nod, as if someone has said to sit up straighter or dinner won't come. I sneak some *haroset,* hungrier than I have been in weeks, and wonder how much longer, as in the old days. Stu begins to sing, his voice loud and affirming, *Ha Gadya, Ha Gadya;* Julie and Alan hold back, uncertain of such certainty; but my voice rises, searching, verse after verse, for my memory of this hapless little goat, bought by the father for two coins. We reach the finale. . . .

> And the Holy One, blessed is He,
> came and killed the Angel of Death
> that slew the slaughterer
> that slaughtered the ox that drank the water
> that quenched the fire that burned the stick
> that beat the dog that bit the cat
> that ate the kid that father bought for two zuzim.
> *Ha Gadya, Ha Gadya.*

Stu is off-key—this isn't how it goes—but I sing on, we all do, each on a separate note. Somehow we blend.

Dreaming of Lace

When I learned that I needed a mastectomy and was trying to imagine life without a breast, I had one comfort: picturing myself in purple lace panties with a matching top, equipped with a built-in left breast and an easy-to-unhook right one, which would tumble out, on cue, into waiting hands. The scar, the flatness, the buckling skin, would all be safely hidden. It would be seductive, erotic, like the veils in Iran.

Even at night in the hospital, when the nurses let me be and that wave of no-one-will-ever-desire-me depression descended full force, I would conjure up this outfit, sometimes in yellow, pink, green, black, not just purple—and feel better. I pictured it, too, when I finally unwrapped the tape that since surgery had wrapped my chest like a mummy. That was ten days after I got home. ("You don't need all this bandage," the resident had said before I left the hospital, but I knew better and convinced him to retape me, extra thick, before I stuffed the lamb's wool they gave me into my bra and got dressed.)

What I saw in my bathroom mirror, door bolted, was worse than I had imagined. I was lopsided, grotesque, deformed like a character out of a Victor Hugo novel or a Grimms' fairy tale: the ugliest gnome. No one could love this, not even Stu, who was being loyal and generous—and who didn't look too closely at things. But he would never see it, I vowed. I would always wear my purple lacy top, or the yellow, pink, green, or blue one—all with matching panties—as soon as I could get myself to a store.

My friend Pam drove me uptown to Eileen's Lingerie the next day. It sold prosthetic breasts, according to the handout from the hospital, which amazed me since they had only cruise-ship and first-night ensembles in their windows—for women with nothing to hide. Yes, they had them, all kinds, said one sheepish saleswoman, backing away. She would get Eileen, who handled these things. They also had night bras, sports bras, and skirted print bathing suits for mastectomy "victims," according to her cheerful salesmate who was standing by the bathing suit rack. Did I want to see one in back?

But there was nothing like my purple lacy outfit. It didn't exist, said Eileen, who had me trying on a prosthesis with five different day bras until she found one she liked on me. It was an absurd idea, according to the scowl. "Wear a nice nightgown. This other idea of yours is ridiculous," snapped this small, crotchety old lady who wore out everyone (according to Pam, who picked me up an hour later), not just recovering patients like me.

"Well, how about something I could cut away on one side," I asked, thinking I would find a dressmaker to sew in the drop hatch for me.

"No, there's nothing like that, not even in this catalog for mastectomy patients. Here, look for yourself," said Eileen, handing me a fat book of warden-lady designs, okay for prison but not a shared bed. I went home with my five day bras, my prosthesis, and a token night bra, bland and sexless. It was a glum day.

That night I wore the pale green nightgown that Stu had bought me: crushable cotton, soft and serviceable. No see-through. We made love for the first time, very carefully, as if I might break. He gave great attention to my belly, my thighs, my one good breast, leaving the other side alone, untouched. Relieved at first, I soon became insulted. He couldn't go near it, even over a nightgown; it was obviously that terrible.

Three more days and I placed his hand over the gown, on the empty space. "Doesn't it hurt?" he asked, almost in awe. "I don't feel a thing," I told him, "except for the tender spots at both ends of the scar." He lifted his hand quickly, but later, when we were almost asleep, he told me how pleased he was that I had let him touch it. He had been waiting for me, it seemed. Damn you, I thought, irritated with this gentleness. Part of me wanted him to undress me, run his lips across my ugliness without permission, and say it was okay, even beautiful. No way; not him, not anyone, not without the purple outfit that I could not find. I kept on dressing and undressing in the bathroom or in my closet. He would see nothing.

The day after that I put his hand under the gown and said, "Touch me." He did, quickly and lightly, again saying, "Doesn't it hurt?" But he didn't pull away. And on Saturday I walked into his study and said,

"You want to look?" and quickly opened my robe and closed it again fast and walked out. He came after me, put his arms around me, and said, "You're making progress." And touched me again. I felt tears in my eyes and saw some in his.

That night I took my gown off in bed, brought his lips to my scar, and said to kiss it. "My left side needs equal time, I decided. It doesn't like being off-limits," I announced, as if I were back in the schoolyard, playing tag games. "My pleasure," he said softly, and made me believe that it was. He still does.

These days I feel more accepting of myself again. I get dressed in the bedroom, don't shut the bathroom door to shower, and don't put on the prosthesis to have breakfast. *That's* what is important, I can hear my mother lecturing as if she were here instead of in Florida, not some sexy purple outfit. Absolutely, Eileen and her crew would nod furiously. We love you anyway, Stu and my friends would vigorously add, and I believe them.

But I am still going to look for my special lace tops and matching panties in every color. And if I don't have breast reconstruction (which sounds like too much surgery with no promise of symmetry), I will wear a tattoo, like the bare-breasted woman on my friend Penny's poster. Her arms are raised to the sky in celebration of Diana and her Amazon followers who would cut off one breast so their arrow cases would lie flat on their chests. Over her scar, the woman has tattooed a band of decorative vines with small buds on the edges, daring the world to look away.

Stress Test

"How do they know how much is enough?" I asked Stu before he went upstairs to shower and shave. In forty minutes we had to be at the Cardiac Rehab Center where, after six weeks of trying to stay calm, he was supposed to climb on a treadmill, wired to electrodes, and see how much stress his heart could take.

"I don't know, but they do. And if they don't . . . we'll be next to the emergency room." He gave my arm a fake punch and stood up, shaking the kitchen table.

"Dr. Stevenson will be there, won't he?" I sipped what was left of my coffee, hoping the local cardiologist who was now supposed to monitor Stu was good. The specialist in Philadelphia had said there was no point in coming back unless a bypass was needed, which he doubted. The angioplasty should hold.

"I'm not sure, but *you* can be there. I did ask the appointment nurse about that." Stu disappeared out the door as I sat—surprised, pleased, and scared. Stu was the one who never assumed problems. The glass is half full, not half empty, he's told me since we met, whatever my worry: love, house, kids, broken hi-fi. So I expected: "This is nothing. You don't have to come with me." I had planned for a fight, of course.

I thought of the check he handed me at Philadelphia Presbyterian on the morning of his angioplasty: five thousand dollars.

"Hold onto this for good luck," he said as we waited for the orderly to put him on a stretcher. It was made out to me from our joint account, so I wouldn't get stuck like our neighbor, who couldn't get into her safe-deposit box for weeks after her husband died. Her son-in-law had to lend her money for the burial. "But don't cash it yet," Stu had smiled, squeezing my hand as they wheeled me away.

It was still in my wallet. Stu had never asked for it back. Maybe after today, I thought, or—if he does great on the stress test—we'll cash it in and head for Bali or Mt. Everest to celebrate total recovery. Stu was still hoping for that. "It was all a mistake. I would have slowed down anyway once I finished the grant proposal and salary review," he kept telling me whenever I hinted that this was his own damn fault for being a hyper, Type A plus. "My heart attack came three days too early, that's all." Dreamer.

"You look nice," I said as he came back into the kitchen wearing my favorite blue shirt. It put some color in his face even without a tan. Anything but gray and yellow worked with his suddenly all-gray hair, but blue was best. "Just stand up straight," I said; his shoulders were hunched, making his five-foot-eleven-inch frame look small. I pulled his shoulders back to make them broader and kissed his neck, expecting a you're-not-my-mother quip that didn't come. He headed for the back door, amused and rigidly upright. "Do I pass inspection?"

"You can come in now." A sweet-faced nurse stood before me in the waiting room where, despite the intercom and nonstop phone, I'd been trying to read *Newsweek* since they whisked Stu down the hall thirty minutes ago. I jumped, she smiled. "He's all set to go."

Stu was sitting in a cubicle, eight-by-eight at best, perched on an examining table, bare-chested except for about fifteen electrical leads suctioned all over his upper half. I was put in a chair in the corner, my face brushing against his belt buckle and blue shirt, which hung on a wall hook. The treadmill took up the rest of the space, a six-foot ramp leading up to a board of dials, digital numbers, and muted lights. Where would the doctor stand for this test? There was no room and no air.

"Small room, eh?" I whispered, wishing I were outside. "Are you okay?"

"Fine, except for feeling like a pineapple with toothpicks. It took them forever to wire me up. The leads wouldn't stick."

"Are you sure this can't electrocute you? You look pretty wet to me."

"No, it's not that kind of electricity. And that's cream, not water." I listened for an edge to his voice, signaling: Don't overreact. Relax, woman. I heard none.

"Would you sign these papers, please?" The nurse was back with three forms and a pen, smiling as before. "Just a formality for insurance purposes. There is a slight risk, a tiny percentage of every thousand. Nothing to be concerned about, but we need a release."

"I thought you wanted to relax me. My heartbeat just went up ten points," Stu kidded her, skimming the forms and signing them.

"Isn't the doctor going to be here?" I asked, sure that my heartbeat was up twenty points.

"Yes indeedy." A tall, husky man walked through the doorway, introduced himself as Dr. Stevenson, and shook our hands vigorously. "Ready to start?" his voice boomed in this little space, "The nurse explained everything?"

Stu nodded. I crossed my legs.

"Here, sir. Hold this transistor, please." He handed Stu a small metal box. "It measures how you do. Keep going as long as you feel comfortable, with no pain. Otherwise, I'll stop you at 165 beats. A normal heart can go to 180, so there's nothing to worry about."

"What's the best someone can do on this test?" Stu sounded as if this were a squash tournament. The day before his heart attack he hadn't stopped playing his hour of squash, even with a "tightening" in his chest. "I wasn't sweating, it was an easy match," he kept saying afterward.

"The maximum is fifteen minutes, if you're in excellent shape. A level five," Stevenson said, and Stu's jaw got set to win.

He jumped off the table; the screens lighted up as he started walking up the ramp, a slow pace—even slower than our walks around the block. This should be no problem, I decided, just as the ramp started moving faster, and so did Stu, trying to stay in place. Now it was much faster, he was practically running, getting nowhere fast as in a bad dream. He started to sweat but didn't slow down. He was leaning forward, breathing harder, one foot ahead of the other, determined. That's enough, I wanted to yell. He'll kill himself rather than say he's tired. Fool, stop him.

"How are you doing?" Stevenson asked, his voice low now.

"Fine," Stu said. "Don't feel a thing."

"Good man." He patted his arm as the treadmill slowed. He jotted some numbers off the screens and tore off the EKG charts that were coming steadily from the machine, while the nurse unhooked the wires and wiped off the excess cream. "Get dressed and we'll talk," he said and left with the nurse.

"Are you okay?" I asked, still hunched in my corner.

"Perfect. I don't know why he stopped me. I had no pain."

"You're not supposed to."

"I didn't even last five minutes." He was still sweating, pale, his shoulders really hunched now as his future shrunk from him. No squash, no skiing in the Rockies. "We'll be back on the slopes next year, you'll see . . ." he kept repeating while in intensive care. It's what kept him calm, safe. Life would go on, he had insisted.

"I'll bet I didn't even make level three." Stu was putting his shirt back on, buckling his belt.

"You might have."

"No, I didn't." He punched the padded table. "Damn." I put my hand on his arm; he shrugged it off.

"So, Mr. Schwartz, the results are encouraging." Dr. Stevenson was behind his large mahogany desk, and we were facing him. A big picture window framed his head, but there was no sky out there, just the gray wall from the next building and a few drooping geranium pots left in the alley.

"You reached level two, which is not bad, considering your heart damage. It took three and a half minutes for your heartbeat to reach 160."

"But I thought you said I could go to 165, even 170." Stu sounded angry, with none of his usual Mr. Cool that he used with doctors.

"No point in taking chances. Most healthy men your age are only on level three."

Stu opened the car door on the driver's side. I would have liked to drive but didn't dare offer. "Well, that cardiac rehab program sounds good, doesn't it? After twelve weeks I bet you'll do better—especially with three young nurses on duty."

"Right," Stu said, unlocking my side of the car. "Sounds great . . . if I were eighty-five." The engine turned over on the first try. That's lucky in this humidity, I told myself, trying to stay upbeat and carry him along the way he had carried me when I was down about cancer. But what if he would die with the next thud I heard? I could not manage auspiciousness; Stu's mood was always stronger.

"Well, at least you're still here," I said, holding back the tears. "We both are . . . and that's worth something." I thought of the check in my wallet. I wanted to give it back—Here, you jerk, I don't need it—but leaned my head against the headrest instead, wishing it were soft. I shut my eyes.

Stu's hand folded over mine. "You're right," he said. "That *is* worth something. I just wanted more." He leaned across the stick shift and kissed my forehead. "How about we celebrate at the yogurt place? We can split a non-fat chocolate waffle. What do you say?" I nodded, glad that the creases around his mouth had eased; he looked younger again.

"One thing though, you pay," he said, backing the car out of the spot. "I left my money home . . . in case . . ."

"I only have your five-thousand-dollar check and some change." I had planned to get some money later from the ATM, sure that Stu never went anywhere without money.

"Good. We'll cash it," he said, chuckling, and buckled his seat belt while I held the wheel.

Cappuccino at Rosa's

Amy was already at a table with an apple crumb cake, two forks, and two plates. "You'll love this," she said. "And the cappuccino decaf with cinnamon, too." She pulled her chair in closer and took some whipped cream off the top of the mug. "Hmmm," she said, "delicious, right?" I laughed. It did look good.

We were in the old Dairy Queen, made over as Rosa's, an Italian café with rose-colored marble tables, small and round, four of them crammed together in front of a long glass counter filled with gelati bins and Rosa's cannoli. The apple crumb was new.

I ordered a cappuccino, too—without the whipped cream—and sat down, giving Amy a hug. I hadn't seen her alone on neutral turf for months, not since Stu and I had our double whammy. Usually Amy and I would meet here every few weeks to complain about marriage, mothers, sex, kids, whatever. That is, *I* complained; Amy mostly listened. But today, I wanted to tell her how happy I was.

"I feel so normal doing this," I said. "It's great . . . and that's a great outfit."

Amy was in fire-engine red, top to bottom—scarf, turtleneck, and matching mini skirt. With her long legs, black hair (just enough gray to be interesting), olive eyes, and a smile to knock you out, Amy could get away with it.

"On sale at Bullocks. They still had some yesterday."

"Forget it. I'm a ghost in anything red—except my red Honda Prelude. Remember how surprised Stu was when I bought it? My declaration of independence." It was nice to be talking car colors and clothes instead of pathology reports and stress tests—and to reminisce past glories.

"So how's your new job?" I asked. "Do you like working with teen-agers?" Amy had been her husband's girl Friday, part time, for years, but she quit last August—"too shallow, not enough human contact," she'd told me at this very table. Now she worked at a teenage rehab center in town. "You look tired—like *you* had surgery, not me," I said.

That came out wrong, and anyone but Amy (who would look good even after surgery) would have been insulted. A golden girl without the blond hair, Stu used to say when she and Matt lived next door. Every-one, men and women, adored her because Amy had beauty, charm, and brains, and she used them to make us, not her, seem special.

"I do?" Amy smoothed her hair and sipped more cappuccino. "I'm fine really and love work, except that I can't turn it off at night. Those kids have such problems . . . it's sad; but I'm doing okay, according to the director." She paused. "And how are your kids after the double whammy?" Amy pushed the apple crumb toward me. I pushed it back, vowing to look good again, at least with clothes on.

Two toddlers at the next table kept jumping up and down, hugging their mothers. They were cute little squirts but noisy like ours were in the old Dairy Queen days. Amy and I would hang out here all summer, the kids climbing all over the outdoor tables while we sat drinking cof-fee, the real thing—not decaf like now.

"Our kids were great," I said, "a big help. And they seem fine again except for working too hard. Julie's back to her workaholic hours, and Alan is doing all-nighters to finish his senior thesis and graduate, so he can go teach English in China as he planned."

Amy smiled. "Just like their parents, right?" She knew us when I was juggling teaching, graduate school, and writing, and Stu was working nonstop to get tenure. She patted my hand. "I never knew how you two did it all."

"We didn't. Look at us." I waited for Amy to say there was absolutely no connection, that my breast cancer and Stu's heart attack were bad luck, period. But she didn't. "Now we've wised up like you guys, en-joying life," I said at last.

"That's funny," Amy said, not smiling. "Matt has been working six-teen-hour days since his company merged with Davis Marketing, and he's traveling all over the place." She leaned forward, tipping the table and knocking her fork to the floor. One of the toddlers handed it back, his face beaming when she patted his head. "Matt will have a heart attack, too, if he keeps it up. I don't need that."

I couldn't picture Matt in such high gear. He was always Mr. Easy-going. He had time for a garden and to take his kids fishing in the creek, and I was always jealous. They relaxed at night, had fun—and we made ourselves crazy.

"He's probably still feeling pressured to prove he's good to the new management," I said. "Once things settle down . . ." Matt had sold his company to a bigger one but was staying on.

"They won't—not with this young associate he has. She calls him day and night. Even when Matt's home, his head is somewhere else. I might as well be alone."

She was reciting my old script, hard to believe. Amy was always the one who said how great life was, both of ours. "You're crazy," she'd say whenever I'd worry that Stu was getting bored, and so was I. "He adores you, the kids . . . He doesn't need more." Neither did Matt, she was sure, and with that I agreed; he'd never even flirted at parties.

I wanted to say, "It's a phase. Ride it out," as everyone had told me when I was stuck, like a broken record, in the same litany of complaints. Either you get a lover, or you fall in love with work—or both, I kept hearing over drinks or lunch or cappuccino. That's what midlife marriage is all about. I'd picture all the old couples we'd seen in restaurants, staring at each other through five courses without saying a word. Was that next?

I leaned toward her, spilling some cappuccino. We needed a match-book for the table leg. "So what are you going to do?" I asked. Alternatives always stumped me.

"I'm leaving for awhile, I'll see how that feels. My sister said I could live in their house in the Adirondacks for the summer. They'll be in Europe."

"You're kidding. When? What about your kids?"

"They don't know about it yet. Neither does Matt. I'm telling every-one tomorrow. Only Mickey will be home and he's working. They'll survive." Amy gave me a thin smile. "Yours did."

"But we were sick, not breaking up. That's different—except for the suddenness."

"Not so sudden." She looked insulted. "I've been thinking about this plenty. Matt needs to decide what . . . who . . . he wants from his life. And I do, too."

"But you never mentioned anything! Have you two talked? Does Matt have a clue?" I certainly hadn't. I felt like a jerk and a lousy friend. This was why she had left the firm last year. Matt had begged her to stay, she had told me with delight last summer.

"You're the talker, not me—remember? I've been hearing for years how Stu should slow down, pay more attention to you, the kids, the house. I bet your hi-fi still isn't fixed." She smiled but looked like she was about to cry. ". . . besides, you've had enough problems lately. You didn't need ours."

I bit my lip, afraid of turning into my mother and saying: Don't be foolish. Don't ruin a good thing. Think of the children. Or worse, sounding like a born-again bride: Look at us, how we've been saved. It is simple—just start listening to each other, being generous, holding hands, blah, blah, blah. Ironically, it *was* simple, now that Stu and I had almost died, could still die . . .

Amy was right. Stu and I "talked," but so what? The complaints, the needs, the resentments had settled over our lives, like fine dust, seven days a week—and we left them there most days.

"Don't you love him?" I blurted out, sounding like a woman from a dime-store romance.

"I don't know . . . no, not the way he's been lately, always edgy, a real grouch. Remember how funny he used to be? I need more out of life."

She sounded matter-of-fact, determined. I didn't know what to say. Amy was willing to tell Matt, "Look, decide," and then live with what happened. I was too cautious for that; besides, Stu never was moved by ultimatums. Luckily. If we had split, we wouldn't be walking hours every day, trying to find a rhythm to make us well, and he wouldn't have made me laugh when I lost my prosthesis—Here titty, titty!—and kissed my scar enough times to make me feel that mastectomy doesn't matter.

"You want guarantees and there aren't any," Stu used to say, whenever I asked if he thought we would last. He was right. No guarantees. I thought of Susannah Whitney, who left her husband three weeks before she was diagnosed with ovarian cancer. He didn't come back, and she never asked for him either. She died last week.

Amy began to put on lipstick, a frosted deep red. I wondered where she was going next, and with whom. I imagined a great-looking guy with magic hands, like the carpenter who came to replace the rotted planks on the back deck yesterday.

"You know, you used to worry about Stu having a heart attack," she said.

"I did?"

"Yes, you said it last summer. We were sitting here, as a matter of fact."

I remembered no such prophecies, just a terrible feeling that I was being cheated out of a life that now felt great. I took the last bite of apple crumb left on the plate—and a little whipped cream. What the hell? I'd be careful again tomorrow.

Changing Lanes

"Why don't they fix the window?" I almost asked when I first started coming to this pool, a part of Princeton University. It was 6:30 A.M., right after New Year's Day, and the place was packed with the before-work crowd. The window, fifteen feet above my head, was open and snow was falling on the locker-room floor (no berber carpet like at the YMCA, no sauna or built-in hair dryers either). But the two young, slim coeds who were changing clothes on either side of me seemed unconcerned, so I kept my mouth shut and changed quickly. If that's what it takes to get into midlife shape, so be it.

Ten years later the window is still open and it's still freezing; but today, at midmorning, no one is here. I hurry to get my suit on before someone from the lunchtime crowd comes. That's silly, the poet Audre Lorde would say, there's nothing to hide. She wouldn't wear a prosthesis after her mastectomy, she says in *Cancer Journals*, even when the nurse in her doctor's office complained that it set a bad example.

Lanes four and five, which usually share a dozen Speedo suits moving like torpedoes, have two sprinters; lane three, my old lane, has no one. I stay away, still remembering that guy—Was it two years ago?—who passed me and snarled: "Why don't you swim lane two, lady?" He was doing the breaststroke and I was doing the crawl, my fastest stroke. True, a few people had already passed me, but after him everyone went by, and a week later someone kicked me in the head. So I switched to lane two, crushed. Wasn't I the fastest swimmer in bunk ten at Camp Inawood, with trophies somewhere in the basement to prove it? Now *I'll* overtake everyone, I thought, swimming leisurely—until an old guy who didn't look like much, stroke-wise, overtook me in lane two. An old heavyset woman almost did, too, but I sped up.

This morning I'm swimming in lane one—just temporarily, until I get my left arm fully back in shape. Dr. Grummond said this would take three weeks at most once I start swimming regularly. And the oncologist said no chemo is needed, just a pill, tamoxifen, once a day; so that's no problem.

I sit on the rim for a while, dangling my feet. The water is cold. My towel is around my neck to cover the slight cave-in where my normal bathing suit begins. I have to remember to sit up straight now. A slouch reveals everything, but the alternative is wearing one of those floral, skirted, mastectomy monsters that make you feel 105.

Before me, a huge, baldheaded old man (he must weigh over three hundred pounds) is moving like a dead whale in the water. How can he be so relaxed, butt rising every few strokes like Moby Dick? In front of him a thin-haired woman in giant goggles is doing the dog paddle. She is working so hard trying to keep her head above water. A young woman at the far end is floating on her back. I wonder why she's here at this hour. She must be my daughter's age.

No one in this lane seems to care about the clock. How can they go back and forth so aimlessly? Annoyed, I slip in to join them. I start slow, concentrating on my arm as it stretches five, ten, twenty times across the pool. I forget about gliding gracefully like Esther Williams on AMC and try to find a comfortable position. *One, two, one, two.* My scar doesn't throb.

My friend Rhona told me that she is getting fat and so what. She is tired of eating diet salad dressing and ice milk and wants the real thing from now on. And my cousin Anna has announced that she is letting her hair turn gray. *One, two, one, two.* She doesn't care whether she finds anyone new. "Don't be dumb!" I told them both with the optimism they expect from me, "You're young if you keep in shape. It's letting go that makes you old."

Letting go might be nice. I picture myself sinking to the chipped tile floor twenty feet below, but I float upward, surprising myself. *One, two, one, two . . .* My shoulders relax, and I ease into a rhythm of forgetting that will carry me forward into new possibilities. I do not yet know about the pleasures of a big warm lake in summer, where you can swim into early morning mists, the rising sun on your back, the loons calling from somewhere. All I know is to follow the solid black line painted on the pool floor, assuring myself—I'm fine, *one, two, one, two,* just fine—until someone touches my foot. I look up, lose track of my count, and speed into an open stretch without looking back to see who it is. Damn, even in lane one!

73

Doorknob Conviction

"It's safe again. You'll be fine!" my mother told me as I stood by the front door, refusing to open it and take one more step over the threshold, onto the front porch and down the red-brick steps toward P.S.3. It was light-years away in eight-year-old time because a man in a crumpled suit and a black cap pulled down on his face could still be waiting between house and school.

For two weeks he had been grinning next to the mailbox, whistling and waving at me with his thing. It was hanging out, white and wiggly, and he was pointing. He didn't cross the street, and I knew enough to walk fast, the way I did when those two junior high kids called me over to the handball courts: "Hey, kid, we got something to show you!" They were laughing, poking each other hard, and their hair was slicked back like a duck's ass, which meant greasers from Corona, two towns over, and trouble. Even I knew that.

For two weeks I didn't tell my mother about the man. Maybe I wanted to take a better peek because my father always darted into the bathroom too fast. I had no brother, and Bobby Berkson next door was too silly. Maybe I liked the hint of danger on those predictable five blocks from 70th Road to 69th Drive—until the man took off his cap, threw back his head, and laughed out loud. Then I started running, crying, and my teacher, Mrs. Knobe, sent me to the principal, who called the police, who arrived during geography with red lights swirling. We all ran to the window in spite of Mrs. Knobe's shrieks, "Children, children!" I pictured a robber hiding in the coat closet or behind the velvet curtain or maybe under the gerbil table where Fat Max and DooDa spun in their wheels, caged.

But it was me they were after. Two men with badges shining marched me out of the classroom, saying they had something to show me and that my mother would be waiting at the precinct, whatever that was. Squeezed between them in the squad car, I could feel the fat one's gun against my skirt, and the red-faced one gave me a stick of gum so I wouldn't cry.

Not that I would have. I was Nancy Drew and Wonder Woman combined until I saw my mother looking scared to death as she ran down the precinct steps toward me. "Are you okay?" she asked, hugging me too hard, and for once her perfume smelled great. I could have breathed it forever, buried in her arms.

"Yeah, she's fine. Aren't you, kid?" A big hand squeezed my shoulder, and then the cops led us up the stairs.

Through the glass, I saw three men lined up on a stage, and he was there, slumped and sullen—at least I thought it was him. He kept staring at his hands that were squeezing each other hard, no grin now, and I grabbed my mother's hand.

"Don't worry. He can't see you," she whispered, her arm around me again.

"Naw, this is a one-way mirror," said the cop beside me, who smelled of tobacco and kept touching his badge.

Under the fluorescent lights the man looked older and shorter than I thought—the others looked like gorillas beside him—and his belt was hiked up about his waist like Anthony, the class nerd. I couldn't see his zipper, but I thought, maybe, that was the suit, so grungy and dark. He looked so mean with those hands turning and squeezing, like he was wringing a chicken's neck. If that was the guy, I never wanted to see him again.

"That's him." I pointed. The cop patted my head, "That's a girl. Good kid!"

"You *are* sure?" my mom asked, drawing me close, and her soft silk blouse felt so smooth on my cheek. I nodded, and they locked him up. "For good," they all said, grinning over my certainty.

My mother twisted the doorknob, her hand over mine. "Cream cheese and jelly!" she said cheerfully, handing me my lunchbox. "And there's a Cracker Jack box inside with a surprise! Maybe you'll get another ring." She beamed, pointing to my Wonder Woman ring, while my father, full of shaving cream, blew me kisses from the top of the stairs. I was supposed to be their big, brave, honest girl, ready to go forth

75

into a 1940s Forest Hills where innocent third graders walked safely to school. So I put on my two Cracker Jack rings as disguise and became that girl again.

Tomboyhood Revisited

When I was nine I played touch football every evening with the boys over at P.S.3. I was the only girl they'd let play because I was fast and good, usually the fourth picked in a potential lineup of eight.

Sometimes it got a little rough, especially if Richie Pear, who liked me, started tackling me, but it was better than playing around the swings with the girls. I did like jump rope, the kind when two girls turned a long rope while the rest of us jumped in, singly or in pairs, but I didn't like giggling and watching boys who ignored us—especially if I could play well.

When I was ten the boys started picking me first for the team. I was still the same player except for one thing: I was growing breasts, the only ones in the fifth-grade class. Touch football became feel-her-up and knock-her-down ball, and not just with Richie. My butt hurt, my knees were full of scabs, my collarbone broke on the hard cement, and when it healed, I left the schoolyard and headed for the stables.

I loved a black horse there with a high arch to his neck and a prance on the verge of a gallop. I loved how control depended on subtle signals from hands and thighs, and I imagined, some day, jumping him over every fence in the corral, no matter how high Stanley, the stable owner, raised the notches. Alas, when Stanley pronounced that my seat was good enough to try, my mother said absolutely not. I would "hurt myself inside" like a woman she knew who "ruined her life over such silliness." And then I would end up an old maid like my cousin Annette (who was twenty-seven!).

"Elizabeth Taylor jumps all the time in *National Velvet*," I countered, without effect. So high jumps for me were logs that fell on the trail after a storm, and even then I fell off plenty of times, butt-first into brush. I have children anyway.

My last childhood episode of daring took place in the same park where I rode. Four of us girls, all twelve, were having a picnic when some younger boys, playing Indian, attacked us and caught Flora Rothberg, who was always slow. They tied her to a tree, hooting and hollering to burn her, and when one boy lit a match, I charged out of the bushes with a stick. I grabbed the leader, a redheaded punk my size, by the collar and yelled, "Let her go!" with such fury that he did, while the others ran away. I never knew where my bravado came from, but it's an image I still conjure up on timid days: me as brave and tough as any guy.

Soon after that I got a crush on a boy with wavy black hair who liked Flora's pink angora sweater, so I bought one, too. And another boy had a nice touch on my neck, sort of like the one I used to hold Sultan's reins so he wouldn't bolt on me. When he did bolt, and he took the bit in his teeth, all I could do was hold on, my head buried in his mane. It happened a few times—once he charged across Union Turnpike, a truck missing me by inches—but I held on to the illusion of control. It thrilled me.

So did the balcony of the Midway Theater, if the right boys asked me out. I couldn't ask them, of course. But when a coy tease or body brush enticed them to call, I got to decide how far and fast hands could travel. This power was less simple than my pre-breast schoolyard days, but it was heady in nuance, like riding Sultan. And it worked. Except for Noel, who was labeled a "sex maniac," the boys in those days of curfews and virginity expected to hear NO and were expected to think of their mothers and sisters when a girl pleaded sweetly to stop. Date rape, when it happened, had no name.

I never became a giggler, like Arlene, but I did stick out my chest a lot to persuade and cajole, and except for punching Noel in the crotch on our only date, I no longer demanded, insisted, or took what I wanted without apology or explanation. Only nerdy girls like Elaine Schultz did that. She got A's in everything, even math, and was openly proud of her brains—but she never had a date. I did argue politics with my father (he had no son), but even from him I would hear warnings over dinner about not being "too sharp," especially if I made a good point with gusto. That warning echoed through years of men—especially doctors, teachers, and husband—accusing me of "overreacting" or "not being logical" when I disagreed strongly with them.

Power, I found out, resided in sexiness. As long as I was desired, I could flirt my way into control. Male teachers were more malleable, shopkeepers more solicitous, if they thought I thought them charming. Even "just friends" were more interesting over beer or coffee if sexual tension was in the air.

The key was not to be too needy. I learned that at seventeen when an "older man" of thirty took me out for oysters on the half shell while violins played. His hands knew how to unzip a dress with grace, and I wanted him so much that I was hardly breathing. I was sure he would call the next morning, the next week; even a year later I was listening for his ring.

If he had sent flowers the next day before lunch or filled my mailbox with love notes, I would not have fallen so hard. The men I loved held back. They would call, but not four times a day. They would write, but not daily poems of love. They felt safe to desire without making me feel that they would overpower me beneath the weight of their needs. I thrived on the exquisite agony of listening to Frank Sinatra while awaiting the call for a date, not the next night, but three nights away. Fantasy required boundaries to define it, and those who sensed that— whether out of detachment or cleverness—made me fall in love.

My daughter, forty years later, was the same way. As a nineties woman with a good job and her own apartment, she had plenty of men calling nightly, or more, for her attention, but the one she fell for was less predictable. Maybe once or twice a week, at first. Unlike a fifties girl, she called him, treated him to dinner, and planned a weekend getaway for his birthday. But like a fifties girl, she waited for his proposal (which took a year in coming)—and the waiting cemented her love.

My friend Rosa, who is forty, is also waiting, but after five years there's no pleasure in it. Her lover sees her Monday through Friday and goes home to his wife on weekends. Rosa wants a seven-day relationship, but she does not demand it, does not say good-bye, and does not find something terrific to do on weekends. At fifteen, I would have found this romantic; at forty, I would have sympathized; but lately something new has happened. I want her to pick up the stick and say, "Let her go!" or "Let me go!" if that's on her mind.

The tomboy in the schoolyard did not camouflage intent with passivity. She grabbed that football, same as the guys—and I am closer to that girl again. She makes me feisty on a committee I cochair with a man who has a different agenda from mine. Ten years ago I would have wooed him over coffee rather than disagree openly. Now I do both. That tomboy makes me vow not to make domestic excuses for saying "no" at work. A man tells you he can't make the meeting, sorry. A one-minute explanation. A woman tells you why she can't get a baby-sitter, her child has a slight fever, or she has to do food shopping because her husband is out of town. A fifteen-minute justification, sorry, sorry, sorry.

My tomboy self is sad when a neighbor says that she is afraid to leave her husband after thirty years in a loveless marriage. Talented and charming but with no job and no college degree, with headaches, back-aches, and rage, the woman feels trapped and asks me where she would go. *I* would just go, my tomboy self whispers cockily in my ear (of course I have a steady job).

My tomboy self cheers those like Katie Roiphe who implore women not to see themselves as victims but to punch in the crotch as needed. My tomboy self rails at newspapers that use words like "anguish" and "frightened" for women who have had breast cancer but not for men who have had heart attacks. She tells Stu no, yes, and maybe, with a laugh and does not sulk near the edge of the bed, dependent on the male mood. She reaches over, she caresses, and if there's no response, she tosses around but sleeps anyway.

And when I complain to her about missing the cat-and-mouse ro-mances that demand restraint for desirability and subtlety for seduc-tion, she scolds that it is a small price to pay for the feeling of self-con-tainment that comes to tomboys who are over fifty and under ten.

Anonymous Translation

In Rindheim, our goose liver was not eaten at home because you could sell it in Strassbourg—½ a kilo for 2 ½ kilos of beef. Only with great difficulty could I convince my father that this "business" was not lucrative if I, living in the city, had to buy goose liver in a shop.

I find these words in a folder my mother gave me, and I hear my father speaking. He has been dead for twenty-five years, and the unlabeled folder was in the back of a closet my mother was cleaning out. I thumb through pages of life that I was not part of: letters about his leather business; notes about leaving Germany; articles about his village, Rindheim, in the Schwarzwald, and others about the community in Israel, where a group of fellow Rindheimers fled—and where my father is buried. Most of the writing is in German, which surprises me; I didn't know he ever used it.

The goose liver paragraph is on page two of five yellowing pages of someone's stationery, and it has a typed subheading: English translation. No author is identified, but I know it is my dad. Not because of the goose liver, per se, but rather because of the narrator's stance: a child wising up his country father to the ways of the big city. I always related to those stories on our Sunday walks in Queens, much better than I did to lectures about how great it was living as simple farmers "with no fancy houses, no fancy lawns like here!" He'd point to the neatly landscaped houses on 110th Street, six to a block, as if I were missing something.

Work Hard, Be Charitable, Be Loyal, Be Strong. These were the values my father grew up on and wanted to pass on to me. I heard about

Rindheim when I was afraid of robbers, or didn't do my homework, or bought a new dress, or didn't say hello nicely. And so did my sister and cousins, again and again. But whenever my father began, "In Rindheim we . . . ," we tuned out, especially me, who considered myself the only *real* American in the family.

The article's prose style is more formal, but I hear the man I knew in Queens, the one who loved eating green apples and debating politics (even with an eleven-year-old daughter) and called family councils with his brothers every Sunday to plan leather strategies, while wives knitted and gossiped, and we children watched the clock tick our weekend plans away.

I hear the man who made weekly rounds, family in tow, to every sick relative within a two-hour drive, bearing recuperative gifts such as my mother's plum kuchen. One week it was to Aunt Johannah, who lived in two dark rooms in a house with a rickety, black elevator. Another week it was to Uncle Herman, the Fuller Brush man, whose red cheeks and huge belly belied my father's pronouncement that the man was "never quite right" since he came to America. We visited "poor Mr. Lindman," who shook all over, and the Zuckers, who lost both children in Auschwitz and hugged me too hard. I pleaded weekly to go to the movies with my friends instead, but that was always "out of the question." I had to pay my respects.

I hear the man who, if I wanted a new bike or a bigger allowance, would tell me how getting a pretzel for five pfennigs had been a big treat in his house. But also how his father would spend thousands of marks on a relative in difficulty, because in Rindheim "it was self-understood to help." Whoever fell off a roof, or got sick, or had a death or birth to deal with could count on the neighbors to stoke the coal, heat water, feed the chickens, milk the cows.

On page five I am reintroduced to Solomon, the biggest giver of all. "He gave so much, he made himself poor," my father used to say when my sister and I fought over the best seat in the car. And I hear my father's old ambivalence that maybe Solomon overdid it. Housing only two transient teachers a month instead of ten might have been enough to live well by one's ideals.

Solomon Strassburger was so filled with desire to offer charity, even obsessed by it, that he took in every wanderer who came through Rindheim. He gave them clothing, shelter, and food even though it meant that he had to walk around in ragged pants. His wife, who tried unsuccessfully to lead him down other paths, eventually left him, and at the end of his life, Solomon was so poor that he had to be supported by relatives and by his community.

My father was too practical to be a Solomon. Families were to be cared for, and ragged pants were for Sundays at home. That pragmatism made him choose the security of America over his dream to be a pioneer in a kibbutz hat, driving a tractor through the melon fields of Palestine. He loved that self-image. Also the one of him as young adventurer, traveling by boat to witness the laying of the cornerstone of Hebrew University in Jerusalem—and almost staying. (The photo of that ceremony, his eighth-of-an-inch face among thousands on Mt. Scopus, hangs in my study.) He *almost* stayed, he'd remind me regularly, again in 1933 when he and my mother, intent on leaving Germany, scouted the communal farms of Galilee for a place to live. But she said no to a kibbutz (she wanted to raise her own children), and then Franco took over in Spain, and my father knew a world war was coming. "Only America was safe then!" he kept saying, again and again, to everyone in Queens—and also in Israel, where he went whenever he could to visit his cousin Hilda and the other Rindheimers now on a moshav, farming by the Mediterranean Sea.

Instead of a tractor, he drove a navy Buick bumper-to-bumper through the Midtown Tunnel; instead of a blue kibbutz hat, he wore a dark gray fedora and a pinstriped suit. But he did put up the money to help other German Jews go wherever they could go (you needed money to flee Hitler, or no country would let you in). And he spent hours on the phone getting friends and business associates to do the same by saying, "It should be self-understood."

Staying married (if you weren't Solomon's wife) was also self-understood. The people of his village believed in family loyalty and "sticking to commitment." No one spoke of self-fulfillment, not the men drinking beer at the communal *Stammtisch* of the *Gasthaus* or the women gathered in gardens to do needlepoint and gossip.

Divorces were very uncommon. Even when the marriage was not so good, people didn't decide to take this step. They stayed together for the sake of the children.

So when my aunt Lisele got divorced and moved with her children and new husband to California, everyone was shocked. "In Rindheim, you didn't do such things!"

My parents stayed together for almost forty years, and they were happy, my dad reminded everyone at weddings, because of two excellent rules: Never go to bed mad! Always have a sense of humor! No matter that my father, as German husband, always made the jokes and my mother, as German wife, was always supposed to laugh. Sometimes it took a day or two.

My father left Rindheim, if not its values, at seventeen. He "ran away"—that's the term I remember—to enlist in the Kaiser's army in 1916 and see the world, away from the closeness of small village life. The same social certitudes that he lauded in the stories he told me also had driven him away. He did not want to be a cattle dealer like four generations of Loewengarts before him, riding the trains from Monday to Friday, buying cows from one farmer and selling them to another, two hundred kilometers away. The predictability felt claustrophobic, particularly if you were one of the 350 Jews in Rindheim, who were all orthodox in tradition. Not only were you obliged to fatten the goose for goose liver and to marry well—that was valued by Christian and Jew alike—but you had to be a proper Jew. The men were expected to lay tefillin every morning, winding the leather thongs around the head and arms to pray, wherever they were:

> Every Monday morning one car of the train from Horb to Pforzheim was transformed into a chapel, much to the astonishment of Christian travelers. No one shied away from laying tefillin; one prayed as if one were in a synagogue.

And every Jew was expected to keep kosher, wherever they were. No mixing of milk and meat, but special dishes for each, with specially slaughtered meat. The village had two kosher butchers (Christians and Jews both used them), so keeping kosher there was easy. But on the road, eating was slim:

> During the week the men, staying in farmhouses, ate only cheese and eggs—unless they brought kosher smoked meat and sausage from Rindheim. If one didn't have enough chickens at home, one bought them from farmers and carried them home to be made kosher. The bag of chickens slung over the shoulder or stuffed under the seat in the train compartment was

a piece of "baggage" by which one could recognize the Jews returning for Shabbat.

Whoever dared to light a lamp on Shabbat, the Sabbath, or come home after sundown on Friday, or eat in a non-Jewish *Gasthaus* was vilified in conversation, and for waywards like my father, who preferred the summer woods to afternoons of Torah reading, the gossip was oppressive. "Everyone knew what was cooking in everyone's pot," he'd tell my mother, who, as a "big-city girl" from Stuttgart, was his ticket out of that parochialism. Forty years into marriage and urban life, he still called her "the big-city girl."

Big scandals, especially those involving affairs, intermarriages, and conversions, could ruin a family, even if the offender moved away. For the Jews, even more than the Catholics (Protestants numbered only two or three families then), it was one thing to be neighborly and quite another to cross religious boundaries: they were clearly delineated and inviolable for those who stayed in the village.

I only knew of a single conversion and he was a young man who joined the Salvation Army because he was treated like an outcast, and nobody wanted to be with him. But I think he never stopped feeling Jewish. Later he was sent as a missionary to Palestine and was the first to offer help to his fellow villagers, who were starting the new settlement by the Mediterranean Sea. He brought them a cow. Despite his baptism, his connection with his fellow Jews was never lost.

My father kept his connection, too. He "converted" from Orthodox Judaism and life as a cattle dealer. He moved to Frankfurt to learn a new business. (Actually, not so new. He dealt in cowhides instead of cows and sat at a desk instead of riding trains up and down Schwarzwald.) He moved a continent away, to a new world, but still Rindheim came along with him— not as excess baggage, but as a moral compass. He converted himself into an American, made English his mother tongue, lived far from the red-peaked roofs of Schwarzwald, and ended up, twenty years later, playing golf—an unheard-of luxury—on Shabbat. Yet where he was going always stayed tied to where he had been.

It was this connection to his past that convinced him to leave Germany while others kept hoping the crazy house painter from Austria would go away. I always wondered about his prescience. How did he know, when so many didn't? Was it really, as family legend says, because he went to one Nazi rally in 1933 and saw Hitler's magnetic effect? Or were there earlier signs, ones that I, seeing Farrakhan and David Duke on *Nightly News,* should look for?

I see in the anonymous translation that there were. His insight began fifteen years earlier when, as a teenage German soldier on the Russian front in World War I, he saw the misery of the Eastern European Jews and how badly they were treated:

> In Russia we saw what could happen to Jews . . . the bent backs, the subservient manner, the need to suffer humiliations under the Czar without being able to defend themselves. The Jews greeted the German army as liberators, but they were quickly disappointed and so were we. The German soldiers had more sympathy for the Russian peasant than for the better educated but poor Russian Jew. We young German-Jewish soldiers, self-assured and with no inferiority complex from living in a ghetto, were amazed. For the first time I realized that what I saw could happen to Jewish people everywhere and that impression never disappeared. It was the reason I knew right away to leave Hitler's Germany.

I wonder what lessons his past should teach me, who feels even more American than my father once felt German. I, who grew up on milk shakes and ham sandwiches, had no yoke of Jewish orthodoxy to throw off. I easily crossed boundaries that my father, who crossed oceans, did not. Weaned on a melting-pot optimism, I jumped happily into a post-Hitler, American world where everybody—Protestant, Catholic, and Jew, in black, white, and yellow—was supposed to blend together like the beige wall-to-wall carpet that my two best friends had.

Let the past go, I told my parents regularly until I escaped to the University of Michigan, a thousand miles away. Let the past go, I told myself when Addie and Dennie from Gross Pointe, one night in our pajamas in the dorm, drinking beer and talking about God at 2 A.M., wanted to know if other Jews had horns. I was their first Jew; they were my first Christians. This was trust, I assured myself; their parents would never have dared to ask.

Let the past go, I thought again while dating Paul, a Polish poet; and Nicky from Italy; and once, Sigurd from "near Austria." And again, when Stu and I bought our first house from a bulletin-board notice (just the ranch we wanted) in spite of the realtor who knew about it but didn't think we'd want to live in a planned, integrated neighborhood of blacks and whites (one-third, two-thirds, the ratio of my father's old village).

My father is buried in sand, the wind from the Mediterranean blowing over his grave in Israel. Avocados grow in the field beyond the cemetery, and roses, thousands of them in reds, whites, and yellows, bloom in the field beyond that. Such a tiny cemetery, exposed, with barely a shade tree for its thirty or so graves, yet here he chose to lie. Not deep in the Schwarzwald woods where three hundred years of his ancestors lie and not in Cedar Grove Cemetery of New Jersey, off the Garden State Parkway, next to his brothers and sister and the small daughter, Hannah, who died so soon after they arrived in America. Some part of him still needed to be with people he'd grown up with—the ones who founded the new village that reminded him of his old one—but in a desert they made bloom.

I wonder what boundaries of his past, buried like the German writing in this folder, he needed to recross before his soul could rest, weighted by kinship and connection. When he wrote the anonymous article he was halfway through his life, my age, and looking back to assess, as I am now, what legacies shouldn't be forgotten. Maybe writing about Solomon rekindled something that only being buried by four Israeli gravediggers in blue kibbutz hats could satisfy. When they shoveled the sand onto his plain pine coffin, I could feel his smile even as I cried, the Solomon part of him getting its due.

I wonder what boundaries I need to recross, and what else from Rindheim I carry besides a love of crusty black bread, Linzer torte, and waking up at 5 A.M.—"a farmer's daughter," as Stu likes to tease. These are private pleasures, easy to keep—not like laying tefillin on a public train or lighting menorahs in unshaded windows. I miss none of that. Nor did he, I thought until the day he died suddenly of a heart attack, and I discovered that he had bought two grave plots (one for my mother) among former neighbors, halfway around the world. He had told my mother (out of the blue, she said) that he wanted to be where someone would say the Kaddish, the Jewish prayer for the Dead, for him every year on his grave: "It would be self-understood."

Improvisation on "I Do"

I had a mother's good plan. Alan and Yuka, the newlyweds, were to stand on the garden deck, next to the *croque en bouche* wedding cake, while below them, in the grass, family and friends spanning three generations would raise their paper cups of champagne, "L'chaim! Compai!"—to toast their happiness—"Hear, hear!" Then Alan and Yuka would make a wish on the top cream puff, eat it, and everyone would come up and follow suit as the three-foot pyramid of cream puffs and caramelized mortar would diminish, one puff at a time. A nice, orderly tradition according to the French bakery in town.

Unfortunately, it didn't work in a heat wave in the middle of May, ninety-five degrees for the first time all century. I had been worrying about thunderstorms and the swarm of bees that came around the last time we tried an outdoor party. The cake was the last thing I was thinking about when I walked into the dining room before dinner and saw it leaning, like a wayward Eiffel Tower, on the buffet.

"Help!" I yelled to Stu, who was passing with an armload of ice buckets. "Get the kids, and get the camera!!" I slid the cake, now an inch away from my mother's prize needlepoint, and tried bolstering three protruding cream puffs near the base. The tower tipped more but held while bride and groom appeared. Stu clicked cake and lovers for posterity, and I kept my arms poised to grab flying puffs before they hit the carpet.

Success. The four of us then dismantled the cake, eating a few puffs as we went and licking our fingers sticky with melted caramel. Delicious. Yuka, who is skinny as a rail but saved by a beautiful round face and a gusto for food, ate four puffs.

"Don't feel bad," I said. "Marriage means improvisation. The shape you count on never turns out—but so what, if it tastes good!" I was being philosophical as we tried to make the mess into a presentable mound.

At least this wasn't a serious black-tie affair with mint hydrangea centerpieces and cream lace tablecloths. That's what Julie had the year before, much to our surprise since she was the child with wild hair who loved ripped jeans and T-shirts. Yet there she was marching down a red-velvet aisle in a train of white lace, her carefully coiffed curls like ringlets in a Southern romance. She looked stunning, like a princess—and that's what she always had wanted. She told me that on the morning after Doug had proposed in a white carriage drawn by a white horse in Central Park.

Alan, the kid who loved clogs and black vests, was more consistent. Long before he met Yuka, he'd vowed to have a no-fuss wedding on a beach. A clambake, maybe, cooked in a huge pit of smoking seaweed like we once had on the Maine coast. This backyard fish barbecue with paper plates and red-and-white checkered tablecloths was at least close—even if it ended with a wedding tower that looked like the collapsed Berlin Wall. The new shape at least fit into the refrigerator, which is where I took it before the cream could ooze out.

Actually, this was Alan's third marriage celebration to Yuka. The first, five months earlier, was in Manhattan City Hall, a day before Yuka was to return to Japan. They couldn't bear to be separated despite our advice to "take a step back, you've only known her six months." We would have said that even if Yuka had grown up here, knew English and American life well, and hadn't quit a fine career as an industrial artist in Tokyo to follow Alan—after a whirlwind, four-month courtship—into our world. She was beautiful, with luminous, almond eyes and an impish grin, and she seemed to like us. But we knew nothing of her, and what did she know of us—or of Alan, the boy he had been long before his two years as a young lawyer in Japan; the one I remember, at four, building fortresses out of pillows and, at ten, charming an audience of two thousand as Oliver, singing "Where is love?"; the boy we no longer knew, even as we pretended that we did.

They said "I do" during Alan's lunch break. "It was so quick we could have taken the same subway uptown that we took down," Alan told us happily that night on the phone. Stu and I didn't go, because Alan didn't want Yuka to feel sad that her parents couldn't come from Tokyo. The real wedding, we were told, was to be in March in Hawaii, halfway. "Don't say we're married until then," Alan instructed us.

"But, Alan, you're married."

"Only legally."

"But legally does count."

I drew my line in the sand. My children didn't have to have the perfect, low-key Sunday-lunch wedding that we had. I was broad-minded. My daughter had wanted a Saturday-night bash with rock music to break my eardrums, fine. My godchild had wanted a barbecue wedding in Yosemite, two months before her baby was due, fine. But I wasn't going to pretend that "I do" was not "I do," not after decades of telling myself that "commitment is commitment" whenever I wanted to say, "That's it! Finished! It's over!" Alan needed to know about mind-set.

"Okay, Mom, say we're married if you want to," Alan said with his usual intuition, before I could enlighten him. "But tell your friends, no presents until March, okay?"

"Okay."

Hawaii wasn't exactly halfway, but it was seventy degrees, with clear skies and no humidity, while New Jersey was on its tenth snowstorm. The ceremony, on a promontory overlooking the Pacific, was at sunset, with a fireball sky and two whales offshore, as if sent by Sea World, leaping into the air. The hotel officiator, who was a tour guide when not a rabbi, was dressed in a white Nehru jacket and love beads from his sixties days. He chanted in this fairy tale setting:

> *Harai at me-ku-desh-et lee b'ta-ba-at zoh k'dat mosh eh*
> *v'yiisrael*
> *Hari atah me-ku-dash lee b'tah ba-at zoh k'dat mosheh*
> *v'yiisrael*

"Repeat after me," he said, "these vows of eternal love." And they did: first Alan in a convincing accent; then Yuka, more tentative in yet another strange language of her new life.

We were standing under the chuppah, the Jewish symbol of home, which today was a flapping gray tarp held up by four poles. Yuka's parents and brother were holding up one side, and Stu, Julie, Doug, and I held up the other. The wind was gusting, and everyone was gripping hard, smiling hard, and nodding vigorously to let each other know, without language, that this was fun.

Over dinner, on a terrace lined with palm trees, we sat in a horseshoe: Japan on one side, America on the other, with the newlyweds at the head. Yuka's mother, a graceful, quiet woman who spoke no English, stood up to deliver a speech she had written; she had had it translated and memorized it in English so she could wish her daughter and son-in-law all the best. I admired her courage and hated my silence, but I could not improvise and had no planned words.

Next came Julie's poem, twenty stanzas about her brother's life, which she had simultaneously translated into Japanese by Alan's law school friend, a Japanese who lived in the States and spoke wonderful English.

> When we were little we used to fight
> Mostly in the car or alone at night
> As your older sister on you I could pick
> Until I was scolded for one deadly kick . . .

The crotch did it. Both worlds laughed together, and one by one, like a mini United Nations, others stood up to toast with simultaneous translations. Yuka's four Japanese girlfriends, Alan's friend since seventh grade, another from Hong Kong, and the fathers, both engineers. Stu, robust with Scotch, joked in English about multinational mergers, and Yuka's father, straight-faced and erect, said in Japanese, "May my daughter and Alan live in harmony. Compai." He knew some English, had worked with American factories on robotics, but he preferred to have his words translated, except for "cheers," delivered with a half-smile.

Then it was Alan's turn. Handsome, with a sunburned nose (they had spent sunrise on a volcano), he went around the table of twenty. He spoke English to us, Japanese to Yuka's side, thanking everyone, one by one, for coming, being his friend, and sharing his good fortune with Yuka. "We share the same rhythms," Alan said, toasting his new bride with a tenderness I envied. Did my groom ever do that as well? I squeezed Stu's hand, he nudged my shoulder, pleased, too, with Alan's conviction of love. I watched my mother, the only grandparent there, beaming in her lemon-yellow suit as if she had no qualms, and I imagined all the other grandparents from East and West, looking down from somewhere, fingers crossed.

Wedding part three, in our backyard, was Yuka's rite of passage into our American world. I wanted her to be more than "Alan's Asian wife," which was how friends and relatives referred to her when they phoned to congratulate us. I wanted them to discover, as we had, a charmer who wrinkles her nose when she jokes. A devotee who can spend a week in the Metropolitan Museum to be "so close to the paintings without having to cover mouth like in Japan." A delicate artist who plays golf. A ninety-pound adventurer, willing to follow Alan down the expert slopes after three days on skis. A shy, graceful wife who makes my son feel the world is his—and theirs—as they stand together in the garden, shoulders touching with each new handshake: Congratulations! How nice to meet you! All the best!

I still hear Stu's mother warning, "A child has to know who he or she is." I hear my father saying that marriage is hard enough, why make it harder by marrying someone so different? Their grandson's answer would be the Hawaiian Love Chant that he and Yuka had added to their ceremony:

> There is a seeking of the lost
> Now it is found
> A mate is found

By itself, I would worry; we are always seeking, always trying to find, and that won't sustain you. But they had added some practical advice, which made me think, perhaps, they knew more than I thought they did:

> In the art of marriage the little things are the big things.
> It is never being too old to hold hands.
> It is remembering to say I love you at least once a day.
> It is never going to sleep angry.
> It is giving each other an atmosphere where independence is
> equal, the dependence is mutual, the obligation reciprocal.

Yes, I like those little things: the smell of a neck, the smile, the curve of a hip, holding hands, a laugh, a nudge, an I love you. All good things, necessary, but not without that last bit of advice: "giving each other an atmosphere where independence is equal, the dependence is mutual, the obligation reciprocal." That is what lets the ME and WE of marriage live together over the long haul, balancing on a seesaw of different and same.

It is the desire for this balance that drives the "seeking of the lost," and what draws us to find the missing pieces of ourselves that we need

92

in others. It is why my father, a country boy, married a big-city girl for her elegance, and she married him for his courage. And why I chose Stu's steady, broad shoulders, and he chose my impulsiveness to charge us both ahead. And why Julie, the workaholic, chose Doug, who loves fun weekends; and he chose a young woman who would urge him to take the job that started at seven in the morning, telling him, "You'll love it!"

Alan and Yuka both want their feet to span oceans, moving across them, back and forth in a dance of their own beat. Fast and slow, in step and out of legacy, depending on the tempo of the moment. And why not—as long as they "share the same rhythms" and keep sharing them, long after leaping whales and fairy tale sunsets are history. That's the challenge, even if you meet in high school at fifteen, as we did, and grow up in each other's arms thinking you know what you are getting into. Which, of course, you don't—so you improvise, hoping the little things that are the big things will save you.

It was Stu who made the toast in our garden, Alan and Yuka by his side: "I wish you a great life together and I make this wish on this cream puff." He popped one in his mouth, grinned, and we all raised our red-check-ered paper cups: "Hear! Hear!, L'chaim! Compai!" A red sun was setting, it hadn't rained, the bees stayed away, and so what if Stu had mixed up the tradition by eating the single peak of puff that bride and groom were to wish on. A new tradition, with good rhythms, had begun.

The New Kitchen

After five months of cooking in a dark makeshift pantry with a ten-inch sink and a hot plate, we now have a brand-new kitchen with everything working and in place: spices in the spice drawer, knives in the knife rack. Even the garbage can pulls out below the butcher block so veggie scraps fall right in.

Five years ago such order was not my thing—even with a mother who complained for eighteen years about my messy room and a husband who has wanted the neatness of his mother's house ever since. My attitude was: This is who I am, a domestic free spirit. Take me or leave me. And dinners turned out, one way or another, no matter what the setting.

But lately domestic order pleases me. The regrouting I did in the bathroom makes me smile every time I walk by, so do the screens, no longer ripped, on the porch. I think of my mother who, at my age, sold our house in Queens when I left for college and moved into a brand new apartment, even if her daughter lost her room.

Why? I thought then. She's lived so long with what she's had, why change it? It was *my* life that was beginning; hers should stay the way I was used to it being. Now, as buckling linoleum makes me feel like 102, I understand her impulse (and my mother-in-law's, who did the same thing). I need new, too—even if it means a second mortgage, which we did take out to pay for the new kitchen. "It's worth it," I keep telling Stu, who has finally stopped grumbling that the old, one-windowed, 1940s kitchen was nice enough. He, too, likes light streaming in from three sides and how we can control the sink, stove, and refrigerator with five steps—and how I no longer leave a nightly trail of chopped onions across the kitchen floor.

My old self resists, thinking of Madeline Roth's mother when I was in high school, always re-covering chairs, beds, and couches and repapering the walls. We'd have to step over books of fabric samples, propped against chairs and walls, to get to Madeline's bedroom, where we'd listen to Pete Seeger songs of the working man and sneer at such bourgeois materialism.

What will be next? I am thinking about my grandfather who, from age sixty on, put on his blue suit and tie to eat wheat germ on his grapefruit every morning. I open the refrigerator with see-through drawers that reveal lettuce and parsley without a hunt. I regroup the yogurts and spit-shine the chrome trim on the cheese drawer.

A friend calls to tell me that she and her husband bought an 1850 farmhouse on five acres, twice as big as their old split-level and in need of lots of work. "But your kids are grown," I say, feeling wonderfully modest all of a sudden.

"We want a guest wing for grandchildren."

"But you don't have grandchildren."

"We will."

"Oh."

". . . besides, we need a change."

So, evidently, did the three couples we had dinner with last week. One has remodeled, the other two are talking to contractors. It's either that or moving or getting a divorce, we decided over dessert. A kitchen is cheaper than a lawyer, and so what if no one cooks much anymore?

I do plan to cook—even with the kids out of the house and a new Tex-Mex takeout opening up the street. Stu and I will even cook together; we've found out that neither of us needs to be the General when making carrot curry or black bean soup. There's a rhythm to chopping vegetables that seems to work for us when we have enough counter space. We sit down to eat our creation and all our many years together seem fine. Instant gratification, I guess, like good sex.

It must be that when our bodies disappoint us, we who stay together invest in home improvement. We can't change electrocardiograms, blurred vision, and dulling passion, but we can buy fresh paint, new gutters, and new kitchens of light and order. We will start again, we tell ourselves. Illusion, of course, but with a physicality that's comforting. My shoulder may still hurt from swimming too hard to stay in shape, there's a scar on my chest, stretch marks on my stomach, but at least my silverware drawer opens effortlessly.

If and When

What happened to my grandmother would not happen to me, I vowed at twenty-seven. She was eighty-nine then and at home when her heart failed and a nurse's aide resuscitated her with adrenaline and CPR. For the next ten years my dignified, well-coiffed Omi, who had made me tiny heart-shaped cookies for every birthday, lived in a nursing home, disoriented and blind, her hair looking as if she'd been electrocuted, her arms black and blue from "falling out of bed." I hated going to see her, especially since the only thing she said, over and over, was *Lieber Gott, liebes Kind, Ich will das nicht.* I don't want this.

The year before she died I stopped visiting her. I told my mother that "she didn't know me anyway," which I believed even if she squeezed my hand after I held hers for a while. It was right after my fourteen-year-old collie (which my grandmother loved) was put to sleep after two months of pain, incontinence, and being carried everywhere. The good-bye was awful. We all loved the dog, but *she* didn't suffer for years like my grandmother, whom I couldn't help, hand squeeze or no.

When I was diagnosed with breast cancer at forty-seven, images of my grandmother in the nursing home kept coming back to me. We were holding hands, only this time it was *I* who was trapped in an institution that had the power to stick pins and tubes into me for as long as I lasted. The thought, even with my good prognosis, was more frightening than the idea of being dead. As soon as I recovered from surgery, I signed a living will, joined the Hemlock Society, hoarded Valium pills, and spent hours lecturing Stu and my children on the need for quality of life. I even rehearsed a last-night scenario for when I had had enough. I would gather everyone around me, look at old photo albums, hug, kiss, cry, and then they would leave, and I would take every pill I had hoarded. Maybe Stu would sneak back and hold my hand.

That game plan helped me, especially during the first few years, when every ache and wave of tiredness were dark omens. The beginning of the end. Knowing that I would not lose my dignity, that I would not lose my power to keep control, made me able to enjoy life, no matter how long I had. I cut pink dogwood branches for my kitchen, wrapped myself around Stu all night, and stuck my chin out at Death, willing to play his game, my way.

But as more people I know begin facing the issue of dying, I'm less sure of my plan. Not because my resolve has changed, but because I see others who were strong-willed and practical grabbing at whatever straws of hope are offered them. My college friend with an inoperable brain tumor, my mother-in-law with terminal emphysema and cancer, my colleague's husband with metastatic prostate cancer, all spent their last months immersed in medical procedures that prolonged only misery. And unlike my grandmother, who died before there were living wills and health proxies, they did this by choice. That unnerves me because they, too, had made vows; it was dying that changed them.

"One accepts the burden of life," says seventy-year-old Fay Dodworth in Anita Brookner's *Brief Lives,* "knowing that the alternative is simply death, non-existence, non-feeling . . . so that one becomes willing to take on all the mishaps, all the tragedies, if they are the price to be paid." I want her to be wrong. I want to believe in people like Betty Rollin's mother in *Last Wish,* who lived life fully—even after surgery and chemotherapy—until there was no hope left, only pain. Then, with her children's support, she swallowed pills from Holland and died on her own terms.

I want role models like Aunt Lil, whom my mother-in-law, Rose, admired for years. "Aunt Lil was right, taking sleeping pills. Much smarter than my mother, who suffered so," Rose used to say, waving Lil's good-bye letter at me from the chair by the window. But a year later, bedridden and down to seventy pounds, my mother-in-law never mentioned Aunt Lil. She had an oxygen tube in her nose full time and took one tranquilizer plus two heart pills (to steady her beat) every four hours, as directed. If the nurse's aide forgot, she reminded her.

What was stopping her, a strong woman who cried that she wanted to die every time we visited, from behaving like her aunt? Was she so afraid? Or was she too physically weak to take her own life? Had she waited too long, especially with a husband who kept saying she'd get better? Once, when Charlie was out shopping and Rose kept saying, "I want to die," Stu hinted at options like not taking her pills or taking too many, but his mother didn't answer. As if she didn't hear.

It was the lure of research, not inertia, that seduced my college friend with the brain tumor. She was a scientist, so was her husband. They understood the articles in the *New England Journal of Medicine,* and so did their premed daughter, who spent hours researching options. They phoned me long distance to have me ask my oncologist which new program—the one in Philadelphia or the one nearer home in Minneapolis—was best. "They should stay put," my oncologist said as soon as I told him the kind of cancer, its size, and that it was inoperable. "She will be dead in nine months whatever she does." Eight months after she started an experimental treatment that made her continuously sick, she was dead.

I wished that I had passed on the dark part of my oncologist's message instead of repeating, "Stay where you are. It's a fine program." Maybe my friend would have had a few months of saying good-bye with pleasure. But I had wanted to be upbeat, especially when I heard her family's fury at the surgeon who did the biopsy: "The idiot said there is nothing left to do, just like that. Can you believe it?" the daughter raged to me on the phone. "But the head of the research program is great. He says several patients are working full time after three years of treatment."

Her optimism was contagious, until I flew out to visit, six weeks into treatment. My lovely, blue-eyed friend of forty-nine looked worse than my grandmother had on that last visit. She smiled when I walked into the hospital room, but only for a second. When I leaned over to kiss her, trying to remember that this was the girl who had laughed us out of freshman blues, she didn't look at me again, as if she remembered those lost nights, too.

Never me, I vowed all the way home. I would not be that stupid. I would never get suckered into experiments, like a guinea pig. I would listen to doctors who say don't bother, even if my family and doctors pressure me otherwise. For they do. "It's Charlie's fault I do nothing. He doesn't want me to leave," my mother-in-law would say furiously. And my friend's husband and daughter wanted her to try everything rather than leave them alone. What pressure.

My family would be better trained. I bought Derek Humphrey's *Final Exit.* I wrote a detailed letter to Stu about what I did not want. I cut out every right-to-die article I could find and made him discuss them over breakfast until he promised that he would let me go when I wanted to go. That was the cornerstone of love as I saw it. To insist that the dying should hold on was selfish.

Stu agreed, but reluctantly. He believes in staying alive at all costs, not out of guilt or fear, but out of optimism. "You never know what might be discovered," he said, pointing out an article about someone who took a brand-new drug on her deathbed and lived fifteen more years.

"A one-in-a-million chance," I told him.

"I'll take it," he said. "But if you'd rather do nothing, I'll support you, if that's what you end up wanting."

"A deal."

We shook on it, and I relaxed, my fate in control—until I heard about my colleague's husband, who was back in the hospital. We'd met at a party a few months after we'd both been diagnosed with cancer. He, like me, had been told that "they got it all," and he, like me, was full of resolutions that if they did not, then "six good months was better than two miserable years any day." He wasn't going to squander healthcare dollars and his children's inheritance just to endure life at any cost. He'd read that most medical bills—tests, x-rays, specialists, surgeries, pro-cedures, pills, you name it—came during the last six months of life. Senseless, we both agreed.

Now he was "doing chemotherapy indefinitely," his wife told me last week. "The cancer spread to his spine. We're taking life week by week, hoping the pain will ease." She was worried, she said, because no one was talking to her, not the doctor, not her husband. She didn't even know what bank accounts they had and where. I told her to ask, but she felt that would be an act of betrayal. He had to bring it up first, or it would seem as if she'd lost hope and was waiting to get rid of him.

How much easier it is to say, "You're fine!" instead of "What do you want before you die?" I had said the former to every dying person I knew, but I would do better with myself. I wasn't going to pretend my life was going on when it wasn't. "Death is just another life passage. We should plan for it the way we plan for a wedding or a birth," I heard in an NPR interview with two hospice nurses. YES, I thought, fortified, and went to buy their book, *Final Gifts*—something else for my family's reading if, no, WHEN, I needed it.

There's a real coming to terms with that word, *when*. As a child, I said, "*If* I die . . ." and why not? Children who don't, do not sleep at night; there are too many bogeymen waiting to get them. Even after I had my own children and my grandmother was dying, I was using *if*. I had begun to sense my own mortality—Isn't that what makes midlife so terrible?—but I never said *when*, not until I had a mastectomy and *when* became reality. Saying it, since then, has made life less scary. I've shined the light on the bogeymen, and they have disappeared for me. I will keep it up. Maybe they'll stay away.

If not (there's that IF again), I want my end to be on my terms. I want to talk about it with friends and family. I want to say good-bye without feeling guilty. I want to choose when I leave. I want help, the way I helped my dog. I want doctors to give me straight answers and to listen when I say, "Enough!" I want my family unjailed, if they bring me pills.

The last three will not happen easily. For, despite the Dr. Kevorkians and unchecked healthcare costs, our society is committed to life at all costs. My eighty-five-year-old aunt with severe Alzheimer's had two surgeries in her last six months, one to remove each leg. The doctors wouldn't give her enough morphine for the pain because it was "too dangerous," my cousin had said. "So what options do I have?" she wept into the phone.

I shouldn't blame her—she hated her mother's suffering—but I do. I want my children to keep me home, on my third floor, with big windows looking into the tops of tall trees. Or put me in a hospice unit where the concern is comfort, not how many more hours, days, or weeks you'll live. Or help me walk down the stairs, so *I* can turn on the car motor and shut the garage door—or even fly to Europe for the right pills, maybe stopping in Paris for a last fling.

Yes, I do have options, if only I know *when* to act. Leave too soon and I squander life that may be worth living, as when I left boring parties that I heard got better later. (Someone has to be in the 10 percent odds, philosopher Susan Sontag reasoned over twenty years ago when she chose radical chemotherapy for breast cancer—and luckily she was in that 10 percent.) But wait too long and I end up like my grandmother and hapless others who get trapped in a non-life they never imagined when they were well and saying *if*.

Yes, timing is everything. I must remember to act as soon as hope leaves for good (Under 10 percent? Under 3 percent?)—before I'm too weak to plan, to resist hopeless medical promises or the lure of an upcoming birth or wedding or anniversary. Or just a forecast for a marvelous, sunny Fourth of July with fireworks I still need to see.

Game Plan

Yesterday a friend told me that she quit her twenty-five-year job as fashion editor on a New York magazine because she couldn't compete with all those thirty year olds, so eager, so pretty. "They make me feel like I'm a hundred and two!" she said, slumped into the corner of our lunch booth and eating french fries instead of her usual salad, dressing on the side.

"You're ridiculous! You look terrific!" I said, (she was my age), but she did look older than she had six months before when she was working twelve-hour days, plus commuting to Manhattan. Her blond hair had turned almost imperceptibly into gray and she seemed smaller somehow. Maybe it was because she had just finished cleaning all her kitchen cabinets for the first time in thirty years and was starting on her closets. Simplify and reduce, that was her game plan. But her energy level kept dropping, she said, even if her blood pressure had not.

Two hours later I was in the middle of a department meeting, thinking I would never retire early like Ellie. The others were discussing plans for our program's five-year self-study report, but I was computing everyone's age. "Who will write the assessment chapter?" asked Jack, a cheerful, smooth-faced man, who was five years younger than I, maybe more (but with less hair). "I'd love to, Jack, but . . ." It was Pam, looking sixteen instead of thirty, shaking her pixie face. "I'm swamped!" She'd been a student in my class not so long ago. "Me, too," said Linda—Was she forty yet?—pleading that she had a conference to run. Penny, our rebel, just turned fifty, was making a case not to write it at all, while I studied the wall of faculty photos to my right. I didn't look bad: long cascading hair; come-hither smile; trim, plaid suit jacket. Was that a freed jailbird look in my smile or just the pleasure that came from being around people who didn't see me as wife and mom and didn't ask, "What's for dinner?"

"Mimi, how about it?" I heard dimly. I had given away that plaid jacket, along with my favorite gray sweater dress, when I turned fifty. That picture must be fifteen years old! "So how about it? Can you write about future curriculum imperatives?" asked Jack, the others nodding eagerly. My God, I was the oldest one in this room! When had that happened?

"Okay," I said meekly, my excuses about editing the college anthology, chairing a big committee, and writing two papers vanishing in self-revelation. Ellie was right about feeling a hundred and two.

Three hours later I slumped into the last row of a poetry reading by Stephen Dunn. The audience was crammed with young women, drawn to the poet's black-satin vest, dare-me smile, and way of making love with his voice. He was exactly my age, but did that matter? He stroked his graying beard, reading of tenderness—"It's a word I see now / you must be older to use . . . "—and a girl with big cleavage and a ringed nose arched her back before him. I was sitting next to this guy in a lumberjack shirt and random brown curls who accidentally touched my arm. I smiled. He looked straight ahead as if I were air. I pictured him with a black eye that he would say an old lady gave him.

"Men of fifty-five are in their prime, but not women," I said over celery dip at the reception after the poetry reading. I was talking to the poet's editor, a woman close to seventy, maybe more, who had driven two hours from Manhattan for this celebratory evening. We were talking about women in the workplace, and I had mentioned how Ellie was feeling too old to compete.

"Nonsense," said this five-foot silver blond, whose smile demolished her wrinkles. "I love to be around young people. Except for Stephen, my authors are all twenty, thirty, forty years younger, and I pal around with them. I've just been in the Rockies hiking with one as a matter of fact."

Indeed, she was surrounded by people, men and women, young and old. A few were unpublished writers, hoping for discovery, but the others included somebody's husband who was a plumber and one of my students, a biology major who had come for extra credit. These admirers weren't looking for book contracts; they just liked good talk with a lively woman who made them feel interesting. I straightened my shoulders and moved over to make room for a blond in a micro-mini. She had my old haircut, long and loose, without the split ends that had made me cut mine to neck length a few years back.

I drove home happy on the almost empty road, with oncoming head-lights few and far between. Yes, my cabinets would stay messy because I wouldn't retire—even if my hair was now ear length and I wore big sweaters over stirrup stretch pants. (I was not like the women of my mother's generation, who squeezed themselves into a lifetime of girdles to hide a few lumps.) And even if I did retire, someday, I would not be like Ellie. I'd be like my neighbor Mary, who's never tired. Last week, at seventy-eight, she nailed a FOR SALE sign on the lawn of her house, a pleasant gray ranch with a huge oak for shade and day lilies confer-ring like friends under two large picture windows.

"You're moving?" This trim, green-eyed Smith graduate with silver hair and polished-apple cheeks has lived on our block forever. She was always upbeat and on the go to concerts, yoga, and volunteer work, and if she ever worked for a salary, I don't remember what she did.

"Yes. I'm going off to Merrick Gardens. The house is getting to be too much for me."

"But you're managing well!"

"I'm rattling around without Mac. Besides, if my right eye goes like the left one, what then? I'll be stuck at home with an invalid's aide, feeling sorry for myself. This way I'll have a brand-new apartment," she patted my shoulder, "with a kitchenette, wonderful afternoon sun, and hot meals downstairs that I don't have to cook. I'll be fine."

She spoke the way she had when she and Mac were about to take off for places like Borneo and Antarctica, which they did yearly until Mac dropped dead two years ago while mowing the lawn. Mary had mowed ever since, making their quarter acre seem quite manageable. Now, afraid or not, she was leaving a half century of memories behind, still smiling.

Now *she* is a risk-taker, I decided at 2:14 A.M., according to the digital clock. Not like my Tante Sophie, whose world keeps shrinking because it's either "too hot outside" or "too cold" or "too far to go with arthri-tis." I was visiting her last week. "You should go to the Senior Resource Center," I said as usual about a cheerful place, three blocks away, which we'd once visited. "You'd have more company and can get a hot lunch there." Tante Sophie's refrigerator was empty ("Food Mart is deliver-ing later!") and the blinds were drawn. I wanted to let the Manhattan skyline back in through her picture window. But all I was allowed was one turn of the three-way switch on her table lamp.

"I don't know anyone there."

"You'll meet them."

"Maybe in a few weeks." Her jaw became set. "I have everything I need here."

The woman who once plied me with *Apfelkuchen* and Time's optimism—"When you grow up, your growing pains will stop . . ." she'd say in her brightly lit kitchen—was now stuck in dark rooms of regret, talking only about the past: "What a grand dancer I was! What jet-black hair I had! How I loved to cook *Kuchen!*"

I will not let my walls close in on me, I vow at 5:04 A.M. The woodpecker has started hammering against our brick chimney the way he does every May morning, and I move toward Stu, wondering what he will do if I die first. Sell the house? Lose thirty pounds and move to Malibu Beach to surf the waves and chase girls in bikinis—his fantasy for years?

I wish him luck. But if I'm the one left, I'll stay put for awhile, drawn to the brightness of my kitchen windows, the way mornings here surprise me—the changing hues of the maple tree, the way hemlocks lean in the rain, the squirrels who keep finding new ways to raid the bird feeder. I might even clean my kitchen cabinets in between writing and running a newspaper for inner-city youth. Maybe I'll hire a young handyman with dragon tattoos to admire or get a boyfriend, like Mary, who is dating an old flame who is eighty-seven. And keep playing tennis. There's a ninety-year-old in the Senior League, I hear. And yes, okay, I'll sign up for Merrick Gardens when it's time (it takes ten years to get in and you don't *have* to go), so I don't end up like Tante Sophie— or her father. He sat in his black armchair beside a darkened window for years, imagining locomotives flying on treetops into a world he could not reach.

Yes, that's a good plan, I vow. The digital clock now reads 6:06 A.M. *I'll keep moving forward, not get stuck . . .* and the vines on the wallpaper blur, the woodpecker fades. *Soon I am dancing barefoot in firelight, someone likes my sweater dress, my hair is shiny and long . . .* until the alarm goes off (Who set that?). Stu's side is empty (Where is he?), so I curl into my own warmth until my comforter disappears, hands pull at my dream, and I hear, "How come I still love you when I'm up and you're lying in bed all day?"

In Glorietta Canyon

As a child I saw the desert as a place of death where nothing good lived, only evil scorpions and lizards with flashing tongues. John Wayne and Gary Cooper could ride in and out of it fearlessly—not the rest of us; we'd die from lack of water and coiled rattlers hidden in thin shadow.

But as we walked up Glorietta Canyon in California's 600,000 acres of Anza-Borrego desert, the largest in the country, I felt welcomed by bloom: beavertail cacti dressed in pink, golden brittle bush, blue canterbury bells lining the mountain trail into the badlands, desert stars flat like miniature daisies against gray stone.

It was early April, and Stu and I had come to see the suddenness of color; we drove fast over mountains to leave a dull San Diego conference two hours behind. "It's magic. You won't believe it," our friends had said, fellow easterners who'd been here last year to escape the gray, damp harshness of New Jersey hanging onto winter. I expected heat, dryness, the clarity of the sun. I even expected the hotel's opulence of red, yellow, and white flowers and the ultra green grass, catered to by sprinklers twirling morning and night. Sensual delight designed to comfort travelers who stop at La Casa del Zorro, the only oasis in twenty miles, which can be reserved by Visa, three months in advance.

I did not expect the affirmation that waited in the dust and cracked clay and rutted gulches, half a mile off the paved road to the right of the blinking light. Stu was holding our wildflower folder from the ranger station and naming everything in sight: ocotillo, desert agave, mesquite, creosote, lupine, checking them off with a big smile. I imagined God going around the earth, naming, and then testing himself until he knew what he saw.

"Maybe my mother was right to take up bridge. It's amazing how she still can remember everything," I said, as we quizzed each other and meandered up the canyon, any which way, not like at home where wooded trails are marked with spray paint every eighth of a mile. As long as we kept between the two walls of mountain, heading uphill, we could walk randomly among the low salt licks and tumbleweed and cacti that hugged the ground.

Our car had disappeared from sight, and I was thinking about how names always eluded me. Growing up I never knew oak from maple, never distinguished basil from thyme in the window box, or zinnias from petunias in the garden. My parents, having grown up speaking German, had no time for such nuances of language. I couldn't name what grew outside my window, and if someone mentioned peonies, I shrugged, nonplussed but undaunted. I preferred to lay on my bed and learn the lyrics of a thousand 1950s love songs instead, which still resurface regularly on WRDR, the station of golden oldies.

"That's a beavertail cactus. See the yellow bloom?" Stu beamed, checking off number twelve out of fifty-eight in the folder. "I am good at this." I could picture him ten years from now—he'd be sixty-six, I, sixty-five—walking these paths, folder still in hand. I kept repeating my litany of names, adding the spiked, stubby cactus, squatting with its shocking pink flowers.

Within days its color would be gone; within months I wouldn't remember what it was called, not without the wildflower folder saved somewhere in a drawer. Like the muted desert tones during most of the year, the tones of my experience stayed hidden in subtleties hard to invoke. Had I not taken home the folder, had I not made a journal entry, I would not remember how the lush and the barren live side by side; how sudden rains turn grays and tans into pinks and greens within hours; how what appears dead can brim with survivors who have learned how to store a drop of water, a square inch of shade. I would have forgotten that the scraggly creosote protects itself from parasites by dropping leaves with a smell that assures privacy and that the desert Indians (their name already faded) took a nondescript agave leaf and made rope thread and needles to survive. But so far they linger, these fragile lessons that at twelve I had no need to memorize.

This was not a place for youth, unconcerned with hoarding life, so abundant and so easy to squander without consequences. This was a world that made do, sometimes gloriously (those few weeks in spring), sometimes not, but always there was life going on in the shadows, out of the sun, and possibilities to run with, like the coyote packs I heard, under the bright stars touching the night Earth.

Part 3: Life after Breakfast

A Map to Cape Cod

We had just passed the Exxon station, our usual point of no return for asking if someone unplugged the coffee pot, forgot sunglasses, heart pills, whatever. After that, we knew better than to ask something dangerous, but "Do you have the map?" slipped out three stoplights later because Stu assumed it was rhetorical. Of course we had the map.

I didn't say, "Paddle in the boat!" because I already said that thirty minutes before, at home. I'd been looking for a short-cut around Providence for our Friday (the 13th!) drive in summer, when Stu passed by and said, "Don't forget to fold the map and put it back in the car."

"Paddle in the boat!" I had snapped and slammed the bathroom door shut. That's our signal, instituted years before after our rented Sunfish sailed into the bay, and I said, "Do you have the paddle?" causing apoplexy in the expert sailor (self-proclaimed) that one, I questioned the obvious, and two, I assumed the worst. Stony silence all weekend. Paddle in the boat, gently said, is supposed to avert future disaster, and if we are on a beach sipping margaritas all week, it does. (So does pulling your left ear to signal, "You said that already!") But if we are about to spend the day in a car after a bad week, and Stu is driving—a man who, even without a destination, cannot waste a nano-second getting there—"gently" is hard.

I watched his jaw set when the map wasn't in my car door slot and he thrust all the maps from his door slot at me: New York, twice, Connecticut, Trenton, Atlantic City, Mercer County, New England. Good enough! I found Cape Cod, like a hook into the Atlantic, and that's what we needed to get to the wedding 280 miles away, on time, if we were lucky with traffic.

"We're fine," I said. "We have a New England map."

"I wanted the Massachusetts map, damn it. Which you left. Typical."

"What do you mean 'typical'?" I ignored his lane-switching fury as I cupped my hand in the wind above the side view mirror. Typical, my ass. I never lost maps. My car keys, yes. My glasses, yes. Five or six times a day, but I always found them. The only thing that didn't show up, lately, was my Visa card—Could I help that my wallet stitching was ripped?—and the damned gas receipts, which I saw no reason to save. I always use the same Sunoco station.

Besides *he* lost plenty of things—his pens, the halogen lamp receipt, and . . . I resolved yet again to start a list, because all I could think of was how he almost lost me by electrocution with the sump pump thirty years ago. Saying that would have turned this skirmish into war. We'd had plenty of those, but not at the outset of a five-hour car ride to a hotel that cost $150 per night with no refund short of death—or murder, which sounded quite attractive at the moment. I turned up NPR's Nina Totenberg interpreting a Supreme Court decision about the right to die, sighed loudly, and took four swigs of bottled water.

"Don't I get some?" Stu asked, as I pushed the lid down again and handed it over. Let him open it himself.

I was counting phone poles and thinking about every man I knew who never blamed and hated maps—when it hit me. *He* had the map last. I'd folded it, put it on top of my pocketbook, and he'd reopened it on the kitchen table to check my proposed short-cut. Now *that* was typical. Like Berkeley's tree falling in the forest, my ideas didn't exist until Stu checked them out.

"Actually . . . *you* had the map last, dear." I was all sweetness now that it was his fault. "I bet it's here somewhere. You *always* get upset about losing something. Then you *typically* (great word!) find it." I resisted using it twice. "You read it while having a last cup of coffee, remember?"

"It's still your fault. *You* took it out of the car."

"But *you* didn't put it back," I snickered. The man was so self-righteous.

Three miles, five miles. The stock market had dropped fifty points; there was a thunderstorm watch for Connecticut; and I looked for dinosaurs in clouds over Newark Airport while Stu cursed drivers under his breath—son of a bitch! idiot!—until a hunk of a kid in a red Miata cut us off and gave him the finger. Yes, I thought. Do that again.

I was debating about being conciliatory—after all, he'd had a bad week of deadlines, and root canal work, too—when I heard: "Whoa! The gas here is only $1.28! Too bad you filled the tank before we left." YOU. Note that pronoun. He was the one who said to get gas while he

112

finished packing. I know about picking your battles, but I wasn't going to be a doormat like Marg, who, to keep the peace, would say "You're right, dear!" even when Jack yelled at her for *not* going through a red light. Last month, Jack left her for another doormat, twenty years younger. Uh, uh, not me.

"Will you stop? Either you forget the dumb map and we have a nice trip, or just turn around right now. I'm not spending a weekend with a loaded gun."

Silence. Five more minutes. The car slowed to 60 mph, Stu stayed in the middle lane and put on one of his three-CD sets of Simon and Garfunkel.

"They always put us in a good mood!" he said, starting to beat time to "Bridge over Troubled Waters."

We were approaching the George Washington Bridge, and I wanted to joke about maps over troubled waters, but jokes were risky; so I focused on trying to remember these guys. Tom and Jerry, they'd called themselves in Forest Hills High, but even the faces on the CD cover didn't help. "Do you remember them?" I asked, because Stu was a year ahead of me, and Tom and Jerry, a.k.a. Simon and Garfunkel, were a year behind.

"No, do you?"

"No."

They were answers we knew because we'd had this conversation before, but at least we were off maps and blame.

"Take out the EZ Pass, will you?" The tollbooth was coming up. "It's in the glove compartment." Stu put the new gadget on the windshield and we zipped through an empty EZ Pass toll line. "Hey, hey, hey, Mrs. Robinson!" Stu said, all smiles as we passed two-dozen cars on the left and right. There was nothing better, aside from sex, to lighten him up.

Up the Henry Hudson, the road was ours, as if this were Minnesota, not Manhattan. No traffic, no price-of-gas signs, no EZ Pass tollbooths to comment on. Hey, hey, hey. I was optimistic. "I love this song, 'Dangling Conversation,'" Stu said, raising the volume I was about to lower. "Listen to the words."

It was a quiet song that I didn't know. Man and woman in late afternoon shadows, dangling conversations, superficial sighs, indifference "like shells upon the shore." I liked it, too, as long as it didn't start feeling like "our song."

There were no thunderstorms in Connecticut, the sky was a cobalt blue, and I was thinking romance and wedding gowns as I overlooked a bay of sailboats and whaling boats. I imagined a sweet sunset, holding hands, the quiet lapping of waves. We might have time before the clambake that was to launch a two-day wedding celebration with one hundred guests, of which we knew about seven. The bride was in Stu's department—he'd recruited her, in fact—and she reminded me of Julie, same spunk and long, wild hair, but a brunette, not a blond.

"We first came here when Julie was four months old, remember?" I said. "Your parents agreed to baby-sit and we took off like escaped convicts."

"Yes, that was a nice trip—and quiet. She could really shriek, your daughter."

"You mean *your* daughter."

Nostalgia was working, the past smoothing out the present. Claiming the kids' good traits while saying "yours" for the bad ones was familiar territory, easy to travel on.

"Only her *smiles* came from me!" he said, poking me.

"You wish!" I said and passed him a pear, thinking we should stop for ice cream. I remembered a great roadside stand, which we'd discovered when I taught a writing workshop at Martha's Vineyard for two weeks every summer. Stu came as "spouse," a nice role change for us, until he began counting his leisure while I worked as "our" summer vacation.

"Look at that truck, will you?" Stu leaned over the steering wheel. Traffic was picking up again. "He cut off that red Dodge."

"Remember there was the best Rocky Road ice cream we ever had somewhere near Buzzards Bay. I bet it's still there."

"That idiot truck should get a ticket. He's not allowed in the left lane. No wonder the blue Camero is tailgating him."

"How about it?"

"What?"

"Ice cream, homemade." Pause. Stu changed lanes. One, two, three, four. Hello, wherever you are. I hummed "Dangling Conversation."

"Not on this highway," he answered, after I'd counted to 1007 in my head. "That's for sure. But if you see the stand, yell."

Stu blinked his brights at the blue Camero now in front of him. We returned to one conversation. "Be careful," I said. "These days the guy might pull a gun on you."

"Don't worry. It's a cute blond in a halter top. It's amazing how fast young women drive these days."

Water appeared on our right, and Stu wanted the map instead of following the signs to Cape Cod. What a fuddy-duddy he'd become! I wanted to be with the boy who loved exploring in the car, relying on intuition as if we were Lewis and Clark. I was the one who used to check his intuition at every gas station, but no more.

A split in the road came up quickly. "We need the Sagamore Bridge," Stu said, "not Bourne Bridge. So be careful." He started opening the bride's printed instructions again.

"Just keep going," I said, hustling to find the spot on the map. "495 goes into Route 6 around Buzzards Bay." All roads converged in about a half an inch of Massachusetts, so I couldn't tell too much. "Just follow the signs to Provincetown."

"Check if there's an insert for the Cape."

"There's no problem!" I snapped. "We take 6." The Cape is surrounded by water, so how lost could you get? It was not exactly like driving in Prague, where we had ended up following a cab driver to the airport.

"The Massachusetts map you left would have shown it clearly." Drop dead, I thought. Back to square one. "Which way?"

A giant sign read, "Bourne Bridge—Keep Right," so I guessed left, and thirty seconds later we were stopped at a red light. He fumed. "You really screwed us up."

A car was turning left so we couldn't go on the green light. He fumed again. "We should have stayed on the highway, damn it!"

Strip malls were on both sides, but it was just for a mile, two at most, according to the map. Big deal.

"So turn around if you want." I shut the map. He should find his own way to the wedding. It was his colleague anyway, no one I really knew.

"You're right to shut the map. You can't fuckin' read it!" Stu shouted, his face crimson the way my dad's was when he'd explode. That did it. I, who guided him across continents, hadn't gotten us lost (except for Prague, which didn't count—and Stockholm, a whole other story) since the morning after our wedding when we circled Central Park for two hours, trying to find the Lincoln Tunnel. I was through. It was separate vacations from now on, I vowed, my hand on the door handle, ready to leap out. When there it was, the red-and-yellow sign with two, giant triple-scoop cones: "Homemade! The Best!!!" Stu passed it, just went right by.

"Which way?" he said. We were approaching a major traffic circle. "Which way? 6 East or what?" I said nothing. If he didn't see the sign for Hyannis, tough, we'd just go to Maine. Two minutes later we were flying along a tree-lined, no-light boulevard with a 6E sign and he was saying cheerfully, "No ice cream stands here. You hungry?"

Silence.

115

"You aren't talking to me?"

Silence.

"I'm sorry. You read maps fine—*if* you don't leave the good one at home. Joke, joke."

I was not laughing. "You passed the good ice cream stand."

"I did? Where?"

"When you were having a traffic fit."

"Why didn't you say something? I'll go back." He put on the brakes. "At the next U-turn."

"It's miles back. Just forget it."

"No sirree . . . we'll . . ." There was no U-turn in sight. "Well, okay, but yell when you see the next stand. Promise?"

Silence.

"Promise?" Silence. He took my hand. "It's been a tough week. I *am* sorry."

Silence. Two more miles.

"I promise."

We had Rocky Road low-fat yogurt with sprinkles in Brewster, three minutes from the hotel, and we reached some dunes by walking a planked boardwalk through a mile of cranberry bogs. The sand felt warm despite a slight drizzle, which blew in from nowhere. The faint smell of marsh rot mixed with the sea breeze as we stepped on seaweed and broken shells, our heels sinking into soft sand. Closer to the water the sand looked hard and smooth. "Let's go there," I said.

"We'll get wet. Do you care?" The tide was inching in, first in thin rivulets, and then carving out pockets of shoreline in half-circles. I thought of Olympic Beach, years before, and how Stu hadn't realized the tide comes in twice. Don't be so timid, he kept saying, pulling me along with a certainty I overrode as the water kept rising. Now that was another mistake of his, a big one that I could add to my list.

"Remember Olympic Beach?" I said. "The giant rocks jutting out into the ocean, and how we walked out under them to see the tide pools . . . You almost got us killed." We were out of the car, so I said it straight out at last. Later, in bed, I will say what a maniac he is to ruin a weekend because of a map and a wrong turn, and he will agree—and tell me I overreact and am too defensive, and I won't agree. No one will extract promises to try harder, the way we did when we honeymooned across the country in his gray Ford. Annoying quirks were still endearing then—my melting Hershey's bars on the dashboard, his need to count every car on every freight train—and were assumed to be fixable with proper guidance.

"But I didn't get us killed, did I? Besides . . ." Stu paused, grinning, "it was all your fault." He put his arm around me. "Don't you know that about me, yet? I'm my mother's perfect son. I'm never wrong!"

I bumped his hip with mine. "I'll ask your brother about that!"

Laugh wrinkles were taking over his scowl. I touched his cheek, which needed a shave before dinner, and ran my fingertips along his jawline, and he whispered, "The only thing is . . . on Olympic Beach that day . . . ," he was kissing each finger, "*you* should have brought along a map of the tides!"

I bumped his hip again. "You wish!"

A family was flying a dragon kite, the large purple-and-yellow wings swooped and soared above us, the rope taut as the mom yelled, "Hold on!" to her chubby brown-haired son. I thought of the kites outside my parents' house and how Stu would fly them into the sun until a string broke or how he would reel them in on wind drafts while our small children jumped and screamed with delight, "Hold on, hold on, Daddy!"

Crossing the smooth sand, we waded through the cool shallow breaks where the sea had come through. In a few hours we'd be doing the twist, toasting with too much champagne, making love in the shower, and by Sunday night, with a little luck and light traffic, he'd be singing "Wake up, Little Susie!" like Elvis on his other vacation tape, keeping the beat with the gas pedal and running his fingers up my thigh. A good weekend would last us for weeks.

I could already feel its balm in the seawater on my toes, in his arms warming me, in the good silence as we watched the sun trying to light the gray sky pink, filling the horizon. We should get back, get dressed, but it was so calm, the undertow manageable—as if no wave could drive us back where our feet would sink in softness, making us take two steps forward and sliding one step back—even as we held onto each other.

There's Always the Afternoon

"It's amazing what you can accomplish before I get my pants on," Stu said, kissing my neck as I minced garlic to add to the chopped cucumbers, sliced scallions, yogurt, and tomato juice already in a bowl for Cascadilla. It was 7:30 A.M., and I'd been on the treadmill, revised an essay, and done my e-mail. Stu had barely managed to shower and dress.

He blames my farmer's blood, three generations removed. With the first hint of light behind the shades, I leap out of bed, inspired, while Stu, who grew up on Johnny Carson and the *Late Show*—no respectable Schwartz, over age ten, ever hit the pillow before midnight, even on weekdays—extinguishes all morning light under layers of blankets and pillows, at all costs. His father, unlike mine, never fell asleep before third-grade homework was done or sang "Rise and Shine" before the morning birds awoke on 110th Street.

I have corrupted Stu somewhat, for he has seen a sunrise. Not like his brother, who visited us on the lake, where the mornings are most luscious, and staggered outdoors while we were eating lunch. I didn't say anything, of course, except, "It's a sacrilege to miss how the sun lifts the mist off the water!"

"He did see last night's moonbeams skid across the lake toward us," Stu countered. A beautiful sight, I admit, the way they head for your feet when the moon is full, wherever you stand on the dock.

"Well, we morning people see both," I said. I did miss the shooting stars, the Perseids showering the sky after midnight, but it's a trade-off I can live with, although I told Stu to wake me next time.

One reason for Stu's slow motion every morning, he reminds me regularly, is because I'm like a Mack truck out of control. Will you . . . We have to . . . Did you . . . ??? Even too many kisses on his neck knock him over unless he's had three cups of coffee, minimum. And no talking. His strategy, he freely admits, is to wait upstairs until I finish ranting and raving over the front-page news and disappear into my study before he has to face me.

Is this marriage, you ask. Is this love? I think so. Like siblings staking out identities—If you're the student, I'll be the athlete. You're a goody-two-shoes, so I'll be bad—we carve up Time's dailiness. Alone, alone, together. Alone in the silence of the morning, alone in the solace of late night. Together for dinner when we are both home, together for cooking vegetarian (too many veggies to chop alone), together for vacations, for some tennis and hikes, and for sleeping.

That doesn't mean *going* to sleep together, just a commitment to toss, bump, and curl around each other nightly. And to be accommodating when—and this gets worse each year—you are thermostatically incompatible. Menopause makes me hot, his heart pills make him cold. The bed in the other room looks so tempting—but we settle for nightly discussions about how many inches to open the window.

Last week when Stu was traveling, I threw off the sheets and threw open the windows. (He called to say he was snug under his comforter in his hotel room.) I also—you figure this out—stayed up until after midnight every night. I cooked soup, I used the computer, I even read in bed with an intensity not possible when I hear him flipping pages in his study (another alone territory). When I did get in bed, I shut my eyes but just wasn't tired.

In the old days, before we found a good, syncopated rhythm, we did try to find one shared beat. He'd get in bed with me at nine, we'd stroke each other's back and thighs, and he was there until I sank into my pillow of dreams. Only then would he tiptoe into the kitchen for Cornflakes and *Scientific American,* his usual combination until his eyes drooped. Other times I'd stay awake by ironing or reading in a straight-backed chair, never lying down or I would be asleep in seconds, like my daughter, who crashes on the couch nightly to be with her husband as he clicks back and forth between Leno and Letterman. I remember that impulse, but I prefer my bed.

I do meet couples who are both night people or both morning people by choice, but not many. Usually it's because of new babies, or work, or because one person dominates, like my dad, who insisted we all follow his plan. Or they haven't been married that long. Or, like my children's generation, they marry after years of hearing their own beat, loudly: morning person, night person, I am who I am.

Not so in 1961. At twenty-one and twenty-two, we believed in changing each other. Long after the honeymoon, when Stu slept late (past 8 A.M.) I vacuumed, unloaded the dishwasher, slammed pots together. If he loved me, he'd be up. Similarly, when I went to bed early (before 11 P.M.), he'd blast the TV, turn on all the bedroom lights, bang his pillow. I should do it his way. Now we tiptoe, morning and night, respectively, to keep private rhythms private—up to a point. Noise begins if I fall asleep before 7:30 P.M., unless I have a migraine. Noise begins after 9:30 A.M., except when he had a heart attack.

I don't give two morning people or two night people much chance over the long haul. There's too much lockstep, one, two, three, four, like in the military. At first they have a grand time, like my friend Ellie when she remarried. In marriage one she was a night person, but in marriage two she switched for togetherness. The pronoun *I*, which she always had adored—*I* need to find myself, *I* need my own space—became *we*. *We* feel fine. *We* have too much work. *We* are gardening at the crack of dawn. I was definitely jealous—Such love!—until it continued for six months, a year. Can you meet for coffee? No, *we* have to go to the supermarket. I might see her like that, every day, forever. Help!

Lucky for them the urge faded after three years. Greg started to rise before dawn to write at one end of the house; she stayed up until dawn painting watercolors at the other end. This marriage has a chance, I decided with relief. Nine years later I see them jogging together on the towpath, but this weekend he's re-tiling the kitchen floor and she's at an art show in New York.

Another friend arranges togetherness on once-a-month weekends. He works in New Jersey, she works in California, and they have love fests in Chicago and Santa Fe. "We would have split without that," she said on her thirty-third anniversary, but, like separate vacations, it's too much syncopation for me.

I prefer my piece of morning and Stu's piece of night, day by day. That may yet change. Lately my morning Eurekas have gone askew, just as my body thermostat has gone askew. I wake up hot or cold at two in the morning instead of at dawn, ideas flashing like neon signs. My mother says she also wakes in the middle of the night and frets over the impropriety of it. I revel in leaving the bed and Stu's steady breathing to wander a house that is so silent. I hear nothing but me, the fan on the refrigerator, and the rumble of water for tea. I tuck myself into a darkness that warms me. I feel like a small beacon in dense fog, no morning light coming in, just a soft, small glow that comes from listening to my heartbeat. Maybe an hour, sometimes two. A hot bath, hot milk, half a Valium, an ongoing list of things to do, and I fall back into exhausted sleep.

I wake long after dawn, full of grogginess and new compassion. I must drag myself out of bed, just like Stu—who now, incidentally, goes to bed before me sometimes. I don't mind, as long as he warms my sheets but not my pillow, and I can keep telling myself that when we are both home there's always the afternoon, shades up or down.

Alan Should Have Rented a Car

Getting from here to there has always been a big deal in my family. Stu says it's because of everyone having to leave Germany fast and because so many now live in Manhattan—without a car. But I, who shares their genes, know better.

So I should have been alert when my son, Alan, called just before we were leaving for a family reunion at an old Victorian lodge two hours up the Hudson River. It was my mother's eighty-fifth birthday, and she had invited her progeny for what she said was "a last bash while all parts were working!" Forget that she has more energy than all of us, still baking Linzer tortes and *Berches* like the town baker.

"Mom," Alan said, "can you drive Yuka and me home? Otherwise I have to rent a car and it costs a fortune."

"Why can't you go back with Julie and Doug? Aren't they taking you up?"

"Yes, but there's no room. They are taking Grandma, Dora, and Aunt Lisa back."

It was late and I had to pack, so I skipped the family logistics and said, "Fine! Just so you're willing to leave by three on Sunday. You know Dad in Sunday-night traffic."

Foolishly, I was thinking great hiking, not family transportation, as we drove up the winding road of October color and stopped in front of a wooden mansion, perfect for any Stephen King movie. My mother was waiting on the wraparound porch with Aunt Lisa: two trim ladies from Stuttgart, eighty-five and eighty-seven, dwarfed by the giant oak door. They had been dropped off at noon by my nephew Norman, who had returned to Manhattan for the next shift. (Three cars for twenty-two of my relatives going one hundred miles north required fifty phone calls minimum, I figured.)

I hugged both women, feeling sharp angles beneath the black, soft wool jackets. Before I could ask about their trip, I heard it: "Margo just ordered a limousine to take me back home on Sunday. I'll take Lisa and Dora." My mother's lips were drawn tight, her frame, like a twig about to snap. "But it is a fortune. Really, Alan should have rented a car."

I knew the conversation that had gone on all day, probably all week. My mother complaining to my cousin Dora, who complained to my aunt Lisa, who told my cousin Margo, who shook her head, called for a limo, and said what would be the weekend mantra: "Alan should have rented a car." After all—and I could hear everyone, but especially Dora (former bad girl now acting like family saint), on the phone for hours on this—it *is* Aunt Gerda's car, she should have a right to drive in it and not pay for a limo, on her eighty-fifth birthday, no less, and with her treating everyone. It's just like Mimi and her family. She always was a spoiled brat.

I stomped off with the luggage cart and grabbed my hiking shoes instead of unpacking. It took twenty minutes of tromping along a trail with orange, red, and gold everywhere before the Right Words dawned on me: "But, Mom, Alan and Yuka are riding home with us! We arranged it yesterday." So simple, so sane, if I were in someone else's family, to be followed by a good-natured hug: "Don't worry, Mom! You'll have a place in *your* car!"

I told her that stiffly, later in our room, when Stu and I were toasting her birthday with Dewar's, her favorite Scotch.

"So cancel the limousine," I said.

"But Margo ordered it."

"You don't need it. Julie and Doug will drive you home, as planned. You like driving with Doug."

She had lent my daughter, Julie, and her husband, Doug, her car for the winter (they paid the garage fees) because her right eye wasn't so good. "Macular degeneration," the doctor had said, "so best not to drive." But my mother had kept the car anyway, much to the delight of both my children and Dora, all of whom live carless in Manhattan— within twenty blocks of her Buick.

"Are you sure there's room?"

"Mom, I'm sure."

"Gerda, we're sure." Stu hugged her; she smiled. Whatever Stu said, my mother believed (he had been her advisor since my father died), or so I thought until breakfast, when I heard it again: "Alan should have rented a car."

Three heads nodded in unison: Aunt Lisa's, Mom's, and Dora's. They were at one end of the only long table in a cavernous, wood-beamed room of round tables for ten or twelve. Two seats down was my cousin Mort, his newspaper sprawled across three plates, and beside him, in lemon-yellow velour, was his sister, Cousin Margo, hirer of limos without checking with anyone.

I feigned deafness. "Good morning!" I said, and kissed my mother on the top of her head.

"There's a hurricane outside," said Margo, and dug into her pancakes. She looked just like Uncle Kurt, my father's brother, and had the family appetite. Big men and women, all gone now.

"You're kidding!" I had heard wind and rain beating all night but thought the weather would clear.

"You should listen to the radio, Mimi." It was Dora, playing the I-am-six-years-older-and-smarter role. I counterattacked, as kid cousins do.

"MMmmm, that looks good," I said to Aunt Lisa, who was eating granola with neatly sliced bananas. "Very healthy. You should try it," I said pointedly to Dora, who was drinking black coffee.

"You should!" my mother said. "I'll get you some."

"Yes," Aunt Lisa said. "And try adding some wheat germ. And some extra raisins. Excellent iron."

I had hit the right nerve, Dora's thinness—she lived on coffee and lettuce—so I knew that nutrition would supplant car rentals, at least until I could get an omelet and return to protect myself. Across the room a huge man in a chef's hat was flipping them into the air.

When I returned fifteen minutes later (the guy dropped my first omelet), Stu was telling everyone, "Alan—is—coming—with—us. Don't—worry. We're—not—leaving—you—here—, Gerda!"

"Alan already told you that, Mother!" I snapped, pulling up a chair next to Stu, across from Margo. I called Alan when I woke up to complain about his not telling Grandma he was coming home with us. He said he'd told her twice.

"You did cancel the limo, didn't you?" I asked my mother.

"I will," she said. "I will."

"Good." I should have left it at that, but no! That was too easy. In true family spirit, I said, "Actually, we could take you, Aunt Lisa, and Dora if you want, and let Julie, Doug, Alan, and Yuka all go back together."

"I'd like that," my mother said, her future in safer hands because she could see her chauffeur before her, whereas her granddaughter's husband was still asleep somewhere upstairs.

"Oh, I'd like that, too," said Aunt Lisa, beaming. I was too pleased with my victory plans to bother about Dora's frown.

"Who's for bridge?" Dora asked, finishing her coffee quickly and looking down the table for allies.

Hurricane Josephine eased, and Stu and I took off in a drizzle. WE had our ponchos, and "So what if fog blocks the view!" I said to our children, who were joking around on their way to breakfast.

"At least they inherited *your* family's genes for having fun together," I said, as we walked on a carpet of slippery leaves. "They'd turn teasing into compliments at your gatherings, and every child was perfect. Not like my family, who held Sunday tribunals over lunch to discuss how I didn't smile enough, Dora was too wild, Mort wasn't bookish enough, Margo, too fat, ad nauseam."

"Maybe it was because they were immigrants, intent on fitting into a new life," Stu said.

I was in no mood for logic.

We were halfway around a tiny crater-lake, a part of the lodge, and every few hundred yards was a bench with a plaque, "In Memory Of—." Log-hewn lookout huts, also with plaques, perched on boulders leaning over the water. One was called Arthur's Lookout, my dad's name, and I wondered who had donated it. My mom would miss him tonight, his jokes, his singing, and how he pulled everyone together. We all would. I wanted to sit in the quiet of Arthur's Lookout for awhile, but the rain was picking up again, the eye of the storm behind us.

At least we had a good hour outside, I told myself, as I filled my plate—Stu was changing his socks upstairs—with steamed veggies and sliced baked ham, cut to taste. I sat down happily next to my mom, waiting for her to say I should dry my hair or I'd get a cold.

Instead she said, "Dora said if there's no limo, she'll go with Julie and Doug." I hadn't picked up my fork yet.

"Okay by me."

But when I saw our kids on the porch and gave the latest travel update, Alan said, "No room!"

"No room?"

"We have golf clubs on the back seat. Dora should go with you."

"How about the trunk? It's a big trunk."

"Filled. You take Dora, Grandma, and Aunt Lisa, as planned."

"Wait a minute. *You* were supposed to come with us, remember?"

He kissed me with his usual charm. "Your plan is much better."

"Much better, Mom!" Julie chimed, putting her arm around her little brother.

How was it that these two, who had fought nonstop for ten years (it took Julie that long to get used to Alan being born), were now buddies, and I was stuck in the same fifty-year family battles over whether the sky is blue?

"Okay, okay!" I said, and set out to announce new plans. No answer in Mother's room, no sign of them in the TV room or on the verandah, with its fleet of rockers for watching the tiny lake on nicer days.

My mother was off in the Great Room, playing bridge with Margo, Mort, and Mark, my nephew who lives in Oregon, smart man. "Dora has to come with us—in our car," I whispered in her ear. I could feel her bristle. Another force squeezing her; she was caught in between.

"And why is that?"

"Golf clubs in the back seat. No room."

My mother led with a club, my nephew nodded, and Margo put down a heart, trump.

"I can't deal with this anymore," my mother said. "You discuss it with Dora. Really, I can't . . . if only Alan had rented a car."

"Then I wouldn't be trying to get Margo's deposit back on the limo," Mort said.

"Nobody told anyone to order one!" My adult self had disappeared. I was again twelve, facing the bully who had stuffed red grapes down my white blouse. "And where's Dora anyway? She was so hot to play bridge."

"The kids wanted her to put makeup on them. You know her, . . ." Mark laughed.

"Hey, are we doing bridge or what?" said Mort, puffing his unlit cigar, and everyone straightened up.

"Okay, I'm off," I said, thinking another walk in the hurricane sounded great. Dora could wait.

We were gathered in my mother's room, waiting for the Oregon contingent, so we could open the champagne and pass out the "So You're 85" album. Everyone had contributed a page—with pictures, poems, stories, letters, drawings, whatever. The album was the big surprise.

My mother looked elegant in a black lace dress she'd knitted, her silver hair dazzling under a crown of stars and sprinkles, designed by my sister's grandchildren. Dora and I were both on my mother's bed, Dora sprawled against the headboard, my legs hanging over the edge. It reminded me of when I was eight and used to tickle her back for ten cents an hour. At ten I got smart and raised my rates, too late. She left for college and got married a year after that; we hadn't been on the same bed since.

"You have to go with us," I said. "There's no room in the other car." I waited for the ax to fall.

"And why is that?"

"Alan's golf clubs."

"That's ridiculous. Why didn't he just rent a car and save everyone all this hassle!"

"There's no hassle if you come with us." I was already thinking that the golf clubs could go in my nephew's station wagon. I'd ask him. Then we could pack our car and my mother's together and see who and what would fit where. That was my fatal mistake: never plan flexibility in a family that thrives on absolutes.

Kids were racing around the other bed, shrieking, "You're it!" while their mothers gabbed, the men talked life insurance, Aunt Lisa rearranged soda bottles and champagne glasses, and my mom was looking at her watch, "We have to go to dinner soon."

"Relax, Grandma."

"Relax, Mom."

"Relax, Gerda."

"Happy Birthday to you, Happy Birth . . ." It was Oregon Mark, his wife, Marla, and their two kids, carrying a mini-cake with two candles, one shaped like an eight, the other shaped like a five. We all sang. Stu made a toast—"To Grandma, whom we all love"—and Julie read her poem, "A Week in the Life of Gerda." Then we gave her the album, which she flipped through, laughing and crying, and said she'd spend the whole night reading it. As soon as she put it on the coffee table, we all pounced. Niece, grandson, great-granddaughter, son-in-law, everyone wanted to know who she was to others, in other times. I grabbed, too, wanting to see what I had missed in her life.

I saw a child with dark braids and almond eyes, a half-smile more impish than I would have imagined. I saw her as a stick-figure doll tumbling from a doll carriage on Aunt Lisa's page of story and drawings:

Well, the trip around this big table started. Faster and faster, you fell out of this carriage, you screamed. Your mother came to your rescue and the parade around the table continued, she was trying to calm you down. I followed crying, too. It was a sad parade.

I saw two teenage girls in dark striped dresses, my aunt earnest and erect, legs close together, my mother sprawling out across the piano, sexy. I saw my mom, maybe forty-five, in front of the light blue Pontiac. I'd forgotten that car, how she'd drive it with the top down, her black hair flying, needing to ask no one for rides.

I saw her at Mort's wedding, tucked between my father and his two brothers, their bald heads gleaming around this glamorous woman in a Jackie Kennedy red dress, pearls, a pillbox hat above salt-and-pepper hair. Margo wrote:

I always admired you as a courageous spunky woman who came to a strange country and developed a business out of talent and hard work.

I did not know that woman. I knew the one who filled her family's homes with Gerda's Creations, as I call them on my page of photos: Stu holding up six sweaters she'd made for him, me holding up four, not to mention five needlepoints on our walls alone.

I saw her with Stu, holding a cookie sheet with her famous bread, *Berches,* which she had just shown him (who cooks nothing) how to make. And there she was in my father's arms, high in the Swiss mountains sixty-five years ago, a schoolgirl smitten by an older man of thirty.

I didn't want to stop, feeling awed by the woman metamorphosing on these pages and how she was here and happy with whomever was left—and there was no one left, really, from those days except Aunt Lisa. "Let me see, too!" "Can I take a look?" "I'm after you!" Little hands and big hands were tugging for their turn as the book criss-crossed the room, until my mother announced, "It's time to eat. We're late," shepherding us toward the dining room.

I was all smiles in the morning. We really were a family having fun. My mother had called before seven to say how much she loved the album (early morning phone calls, like travel plans, are a family affliction); last night's family dinner had been delicious; and Dora and I had actually talked (I told her she could go home in either car, and she admitted I'd been a cute brat).

I was serving myself French toast, thinking Stu and I would take another walk, pack the cars, and leave in caravan by three—it was all set—when Margo bounded over.

"We already put Aunt Gerda's and Aunt Lisa's luggage in your car."

"You what?"

"Yup. It's all set." She beamed. I was amazed. Was my mother still that afraid we'd leave her here?

"Who let you into our car? It's locked."

"Oh, Mort tipped the valet. No problem."

I pushed past her, thinking, be calm, be charming, six more hours to go. It's do-able, even among these lunatics. I headed, French toast in hand, for my mother, who was again wedged between Aunt Lisa and Dora, all looking grim.

"I don't want to go antiquing." My mother was brittle with worry in a world she could not control.

"Who is going antiquing?" I snapped. "No one!"

"Alan said he wanted to go antiquing on the way home." Mom started to cry, and I started yelling.

"For God's sake, no one is going antiquing. Will you just stop getting excited! My God."

Then I heard it again, someone whispering, "Alan should have rented a car."

"I'm so glad you have such a calming influence, Dora." It was Stu to my rescue. My white knight, the reason I married him. I stormed to the other end of the table, where Alan, engrossed in Yuka, was eating pineapple, a plateful.

"What the hell is going on?" I asked.

He held up a brochure: Antiquing. "I thought maybe one car could go antiquing with those who want to do it, and the other could go straight home."

I glared at my child, thinking: Where are you, Dad, who, like Moses, led the family out of Germany? You could get us home, I know it—and without all this crap, because your two cents was more powerful than anyone's. My mother was trembling, and I tried to think of a joke, the way my father used to after yelling, his face red, and then minutes later, a smile.

"Everything is fine!" I said dully, hugging her—When did she become so small?—and grabbed the brochure with its unnerving list of new options. My son, God bless him, was—is—still sweet, handsome, and charming, but my family was right for once: Alan should have rented a car.

The Other Redhead and Me

It's back on my desk again, the flyer with its smooth sheen of optimism, inviting me to a regional conference on breast cancer. It arrives by mail every year, and every year I see it and squirm.

Not that first year. In 1988, six weeks after my mastectomy, I was feeling pretty good and a conference on the latest advances sounded promising. Breast cancer, I decided after surgery, was not that bad. Yes, I had lost a breast and hated the scarred emptiness, but my doctor, whom I trusted, had said that I didn't need chemotherapy, Stu was supportive ("It's like making love with two women, what's bad about that?"), and I never wore a bikini anyway.

My confidence soared when we entered a giant room filled with two hundred people, mostly women over forty, who were chatting around giant coffee urns like old friends. "Everyone looks so healthy," I told Stu. There was no doom and gloom here, no hysteria, just as I suspected. The media really did hype women's hysteria with article headlines like "Victims in Terror" and "The Anguish of Women with Breast Cancer."

"You stay and read. I'm going to talk to people," I told Stu, as he eyed a table of pamphlets under a Reach for Recovery banner, "Breast Cancer: Facts & Figures," "Cancer-related Check-ups," "A Call for Help."

Over by the display of bathing suits and prostheses, an elegant red-headed woman in a charcoal pantsuit was thumbing through a bathing-suit rack of high-cut mastectomy designs. I started thumbing, too. Not that I planned to buy one. Someone said I could sew a pocket into my normal suit.

I smiled. "Your first conference?"

"My third," the redheaded woman said, holding up a silky blue print. I liked her hair color, auburn like mine, and that shade of blue was good on me, too. She smiled. "I've been on chemo for three years and I'm thinking it might be too much. One of these workshops might tell me."

"Three years?" I stepped back. That's absurd.

"Yes. My doctor wants to keep me on it." Her voice sounded casual. "But I don't like the tiny blood clots under my skin. And my hair isn't growing back." She held a purple bathing suit to her chest and turned toward the mirror, tilting her head.

I saw freckles, not clots, on her hands and wrists. Was that beautiful hair really a wig? "My doctor, Mark Grummond, at Columbia Presbyterian is terrific, very understanding. Maybe you need another opinion," I said. I kept pressing. "You should call him." I noticed her wedding band. "Maybe your husband could drive you." I wanted her to whip out a pen and paper and write down my great advice, but she was admiring a velour two-piece.

"My husband had a nervous breakdown. He still hasn't recovered, although he is home from the sanatorium."

"That can't be!" I blurted out and felt myself tailspin, the way I had when I saw a blotch on my thigh the week before; I was sure it was melanoma. I smiled, planning my escape. "I hope you get your answers."

"You, too."

She turned back to the rack, selecting a pink print with a sarong top, while I fled to the table of mini-muffins being served on huge silvery platters. Stu was there not talking to anyone, smart man. I told him about the three years of chemotherapy, the nervous breakdown, the deep worry lines I hadn't seen because I liked auburn hair, which really was a wig.

"Still, she's coping—or she'd be at home, wringing her hands like her husband." My husband took a poppy-seed muffin the size of a very fat cherry.

"But she should be finding another doctor, not a bathing suit," I snapped.

Beside us two trim women in tight blue-white perms—they could be sisters—were chatting with a tall woman in a straw hat covered with paper flowers. I could not see her face, but she laughed from her belly as a bran muffin disappeared under the wide brim. "Have one," Stu said, holding bran and lemon poppy muffins in his palm. "They're both good."

"No!" I was furious. I wanted the redheaded woman's life to really be under control, not the pretense of a wig and a smile. I thought of my mother always prepping me to SMILE: people don't like sour faces, especially on a girl. "You'll feel better," she'd say, which would make me scowl more. The pressure of cheerfulness always got me down. I'm a dud on New Year's Eve.

The bell rang for the workshops; we headed for breast reconstruction, first ballroom on the right. The speaker was a plastic surgeon, very upbeat, who showed videos and slides about what could be done. Forty of us were scattered in a cavernous room of red velvet chairs under chandeliers glittering in celebration. The building was a wedding palace most days.

"I can have sixteen-year-old breasts again, no sag," I whispered to Stu. "If only my other one looked like that. I do like symmetry." He squeezed my hand, and I looked for the redheaded woman, who wasn't there.

Three seats over sat a pretty young woman, not more than twenty-five, with long blond hair, definitely her own. I resisted looking at her chest; she must be here with a mother or grandmother who was somewhere else.

Behind her, nearer to me, sat a husky, moon-faced woman with a large mole on her cheek, my age. Now *she* looks as if she's had cancer, I thought. She was solemn, no smile, not even a scarf to cover the inch of gray-black bristle on her head. She had on a man's shirt, loose, and was taking lots of notes on a yellow legal pad. She stopped to interrupt the speaker: "Aren't these implants cancer producing? A new report says that . . ."

"I use only saline-filled molds," the doctor said quickly. "Perfectly safe."

"Bull!" I heard behind me. I knew it was the woman with the mole without turning around.

"How long until the scars fade?" It was a buxom woman, mid-forties, to my left. She had on a red suit and a red-plaid turban. Nice hat.

"We have excellent luck with that. Most women say they don't notice them after awhile."

"Even with keloids? My scar is so red." It was the pretty blond woman. Damn, I thought. She wasn't much older than Julie. How could that be?

"We've had good luck. Believe me."

"Bull!" I heard again, louder this time. The young blond turned around to stare, and bodies shifted as cynicism made us all ugly again.

At lunch we were directed to a large round table for ten in a room of twenty such tables. I was hoping the woman in a flowering caftan and turban—tall, noble, powerful—would sit next to me, but I got the "Bull" woman.

Across the table a thin, high-pitched woman was chattering about low-fat recipes that she was gathering into a cookbook. She'd be happy to send us all one. "George here wants me busy, right sweetie? He won't allow me to be sad." She looked at a small, dimple-cheeked fellow eating black olives off the relish tray. "He says that once you let sadness start, it keeps growing and will take you over."

She beamed, and I shivered. Susan Sontag was right in her book *Illness as Metaphor*. It was cancer growing in that metaphor, not sadness, as if the wrong mood could do you in. And if it did, it was your own damn fault, according to George and the self-help book the woman was now recommending, on and on, gaily. "Dr. Siegel saved my life, didn't he, sweetheart? It's so amazing how the mind rules the body. That's the secret, you know."

She giggled, and I scowled, thinking how often I'd wept, looking in the mirror lately. And how the night before Stu had lassoed my naked waist from behind, kissing my neck, then the tears, and whispering I smelled good.

I stared at the chef salad, the tears coming again.

"These rolls are better than they look." The woman with the mole passed me the bread basket. "Usually institution food stinks."

"No, thanks, really. I'm watching it."

She shrugged, rearranging her yellow pad, half covered by a napkin, on her lap. "You on chemo? That'll put the pounds on you. It did me."

"Really? I thought you lost weight with it." I had visions of wasting away even though my friend Doreen looked fine.

"Yeah, I put on twelve pounds in six months." She spread her roll with the fake butter; they had announced its purity over the loudspeaker. "But I don't care. No one else is sharing my bed lately. My lover left when I lost my hair. Dumb, right? The breast didn't seem to matter."

I touched Stu's arm, but he was involved with a woman in a Navy uniform on his right, and opposite me George's wife was urging everyone into yoga therapy. "Have you been off chemo long?" I asked dutifully. She was on another roll, spreading fake butter with a vengeance.

"A month now, but I gained last time, too."

"You had it twice?"

"Yeah, ten years ago, but this time the lump was benign. I did chemo just to be safe."

That sounded insane, but I was through crusading on doctors. Mine, I told myself, knew what he was doing. I concentrated on cutting salad. The loudspeaker went on: "Our egg-free custard is approved by the Cancer Nutrition Society. Enjoy, ladies." Stu stopped talking to the Navy woman. "Interesting lady," he told me. She was going to reenlist for another five years and then open up a motel in Delray Beach with her brother-in-law. It was on the bend where that good fish restaurant was, the one with the great Caribbean chowder. The Navy woman over-heard his enthusiasm and winked. "She just made a down payment."

"How long ago did she have cancer?" I hated asking, but it was a reflex around here.

"Six months ago, but she's like you. In good shape."

I was silent.

He kept on. "She went to the workshop on chemotherapy and said the speaker was recommending it for everyone. New findings from the National Cancer Institute. She was calling her doctor tomorrow."

"Well, I'm not calling anyone," I snapped. "Grummond knows what he's doing. He's head of the program, isn't he?"

Someone put coffee and the egg-free custard in front of me. I pushed it toward Stu. "It's approved by our cancer nutritionists," the waiter said proudly. I was desperate to go. I should have gone to clean two months of junk mail out of my office, not come to this disaster. "If Grummond thought I needed chemotherapy he would have said so." I tipped the coffee cup, which flooded the saucer.

"No one said you should call Grummond," Stu said evenly. No bait-ing him today.

The legal pad was now propped against the table and the woman with the mole was writing in big, sprawling letters; I tried to read it.

> . . . The redheaded woman next to me is acting like she shouldn't be here. But who the hell should? She keeps hang-ing on to her husband's arm, like he could save her . . . And she smiles a lot. Must be scared to death.

Scared and smiling, me? I'd been Joan of Arc before today, convinced that if I burned at the stake, it would be a fearless spectacle to the end. But that was when Grummond knew everything, I didn't have choices, and Death wasn't sitting in every chair in the room.

"Okay, I'll call Grummond tomorrow," I said, reaching for Stu's arm. I stopped. "I don't want you blaming me later—If only she did this! What was she thinking of?"

"No one is blaming you."

"Not now, but you will. Nothing bad can just happen."

The woman stopped writing and looked up. "The healthy sons of bitches need a reason, right?" She grinned.

I looked at her pad, thinking we could join forces. I needed some no-nonsense fury. "You a writer?" I asked.

"This? No. I just like reading it over at night. Life doesn't suck as much because everybody's got problems, right?" She stood up to go, patting my shoulder. I was surprised at how short she was. "Well, hang in there. I'm going to check out macrobiotic counseling, see what voodoo they offer." She laughed. "Take care."

"You, too." I expected a brisk walk, but she moved slowly with a slight limp, and I stood up quickly to go. I was through with cancer. All I wanted was the blue chair of my living room, a little Mozart, and light streaming in through the window.

On our way out, I saw the other redheaded woman in her charcoal pantsuit. She was sitting next to the doctor who lectured on breast reconstruction. She was listening intently while he did the talking, and she smiled just as I pointed her out to Stu. "You're right, you'd never know. They could be on a date," he said, taking my arm as we walked through the double glass doors.

Dr. Grummond insisted that I didn't need chemotherapy. So did one out of two second opinions, so I picked the advice I wanted to hear and guessed right. I'm here twelve years later, and now I am deciding whether to stop taking tamoxifen and to start estrogen so my bones won't crumble and my heart won't collapse in ten years. My gynecologist is for it, my new oncologist says don't risk it, and my surgeon, Dr. Grummond, who was my old fountain of wisdom, quit treating women with breast cancer and is working in a VA hospital.

There will be an array of new answers at this year's conference on breast cancer, but I still won't go. Too risky. Too many lives that could shatter my illusion that cancer and death are distant cousins, barely related. "Look at me, I'm fine!" I assure women who find a lump and call me for advice, gathering stories so they can feel in control. I tell them about my friend Doreen, who had ten malignant nodes and a year of chemotherapy three years before me. She's fine. And about my colleague Betsy, who had a double mastectomy two years before that. Fine. And about my college roommate's mother, who lost a breast at thirty-five and just celebrated her eighty-fifth birthday.

These good stories need to be the norm, nothing unusual, just what happens to we women who cope. Then the faded scar, the ache that lingers after a hot shower, even the unlucky stories hovering beneath a wig, a smile, or an angry "Bull!" fade into daily life—I am again a woman who just made a recipe for cream of pear soup (with tofu) and is looking for a new bathing suit in black velour with a built-in prosthesis I won't have to sew in.

Under the Sunblock

I am not a birder, sun lover, snorkeler, or boat woman, but when our friends said in mid-July, "Let's go to the Galapagos Islands next Christmas," I said, "Why not? Great idea!" Maybe it's because I didn't know where they are: six hundred miles into the middle of nowhere, west of Ecuador, south of Honduras, an archipelago of tiny dots curved on the equator. Or because, after reading Darwin's autobiography, I liked the idea of going where he had looked at the beaks of finches and formed his theory of evolution. Or because I again needed to be the kid who enters the dark woods behind the house with Bobby Berkson, saying, "Let's see if we are smart and brave enough to come back alive!"

Whatever. As soon as Stu and I signed the check (and insurance disclaimer) allowing us to spend six nights on board a small, motorized sailboat that travels the Galapagos Islands by night so we can hike and snorkel by day, we became Lewis and Clark and Chris Columbus rolled into one. So what if I kept meeting people who said, "Oh, you'll love it! I did!" followed by *their* survival strategies for *my* wild adventure.

Bring a broad-brimmed hat with a leather-thong tie, the equatorial sun is fierce, they said with glee. (I called the eight hundred number of Travelsmith that night.) Bring SPF 45 sunblock, tubes of it, the kind that doesn't wash off in the ocean. And remember the Pacific can get rough, so bring Thermaderm patches to wear behind your ear or wristbands that cure seasickness by acupressure. I bought both. And remember not to drink the water, don't even use ice cubes, and just in case bring Imodium for diarrhea, or Lomotil (you'll need a doctor's prescription for that)—and Cipro, an antibiotic, in case Lomotil doesn't work. I bought all three. I, aging adventuress, would be very prepared. Survival of the fittest, on this trip, could mean the one who can squeeze Skippy peanut butter into a clear tube (the guy at the camping store suggested that).

Everyone looks prepared, I decide in the lobby of the Hilton Hotel in Quito, Ecuador, where our group of twelve has gathered. We come from New Jersey, Illinois, Texas, New Hampshire, Connecticut, and California, two via a canoe trip in the rain forests. "It was amazing!" says a fortyish blond from Los Angeles, who looks as if she stepped off a cruise ship, not a canoe. "Inspiring," says a gray-haired, straight-backed woman from Dallas, who is wearing nylon pants that unzip into shorts. Very clever. You needed yellow fever and malaria shots for the rain forests (not just typhoid, tetanus, and hepatitis A, B, C), which is why, aside from visions of boa constrictors, I happily skipped that Wilderness Travel option.

Quito sits on a narrow plateau under two volcanoes, one on yellow alert, says Pablo, our Ecuadorian tour guide. But not to worry, it has been that way for months. Worry more about altitude sickness, he says. At ninety-two hundred feet your brain can swell from lack of oxygen. "I have acetazolamide pills for that!" says a short, hefty woman in my Travelsmith straw hat. Behind her is a tall, bearded man with a two-water-bottle belt, one for each hip. Why didn't I think of that? I touch my water bottle (filled in New Jersey) and notice that he also has a hat with vent holes "to let the wind go through," he says. Damn, I mutter, tightening my leather thong.

One hundred and fifty of us are on a small pier, trying to figure out which of the five boats in the cove will be ours. "I'd hate a big ship like that," I tell Stu and our friends, Eleanor and Marty, from New Hampshire. I'm pointing to a giant cruise ship and the horde of Cornell University alumni with name tags, waiting to board it. They'd been on our plane, one of two that land daily to deposit tourists on assorted boat-hotels for cruising the fifty or so tiny volcanic islands that make up the Galapagos.

"One of your former students could be in that group," says Eleanor. Marty's head retreats into his neck like the giant tortoise for which the Galapagos were named. "Hope not. I'm on vacation." Marty used to teach at Cornell.

"Those big cruise boats are smoother in big waves."

"What's the weather forecast?"

"Look! They're all wearing life jackets!"

"Are there sharks here?"

So goes the conversation as we watch the *pangas* (the local word for a small, motorized dinghy) load people and luggage—on to our respective adventures.

It's like a quaint country inn, I tell myself once on board our *Samba*, the smallest boat in the cove. So what if Stu says it is a converted fishing boat. The outside deck has a large wooden table surrounded by blue cushioned benches where, I decide, I can sleep if it gets too rough below. Inside is a cozy, wood-paneled room with another large wooden table where we will eat, family style, for six days. The food will be surprisingly delicious—fresh fish bought from passing fishing boats; fresh mangos, papayas, passion fruits in exotic combinations of juice and salads; desalinated water that makes every drink safe; fresh vegetables, all stored under the blue cushions—and perfectly prepared by Walter, a young Ecuadorian whom everyone wants to take home so he can open a restaurant close by. No one has anticipated such culinary luck, so the young California husband is passing out Pringles chips and salsa dip (he brought a week's worth of junk food, just in case), as duffels and backpacks disappear below and we follow, settling in.

We are off to see the blue-footed boobies, Pablo says, and the twelve-year-old from Chicago, daughter of tall, bearded Ben and the quiet, brown-haired librarian, claps her hands. The boobies are famous for their turquoise feet that match the ocean color here but also, I suspect, because of their name. Everyone likes saying "boobie," which means dummy—that's what the Spanish sailors thought of the silly birds dancing like clowns, *bobos,* on the ship's hull. But "boobie" also means breasts, already spotted by Stu and Marty on the front deck, bulging out of the bikinis of the two California women. One is married with an eight-month-old baby at home, one is a divorcée named Rhona, Stu announces after lunch (give him ten minutes and he'll find out any woman's life), while Eleanor and I are debating, much to the men's consternation, whether their breasts are implants. Stu and Marty go for another look. "I Love Boobies" T-shirts were a big seller at the Galapagos Airport, although Stu bought the less obvious one that reads, "Blue-Footed Boobie." It has a bird on it, at least.

On a beach of browns and blacks, life is everywhere, but we almost don't notice. Sea lions lie like boulders strewn on the beach. Black marine iguanas squat like midget tyrannosauruses on black lava rock. Only the bright red crabs, hundreds of them clinging to the wet black rocks, stand out. Cameras click away in amazement at how nothing gets out of our way. I almost step on a sea lion tail, walk inches away from a deep red-and-black iguana, and climb up to a cliff to peer into the nest of a blue-footed boobie shading her baby chick. No fear from them, and it's infectious. Stu strolls around two giant iguanas as if they were fake. "That's because there are few predators on this island," Pablo explains, and points out a Galapagos hawk circling above. "That's the main one here."

We walk single file on the narrow dirt trail and are warned not to take anything and to stay on the trail. The Ecuadorians want desperately to keep this world as is, a hard task given the sixty thousand tourists who walk here yearly, trying to imagine life without themselves. Unfortunately even the "greenest" among them tromp in deep-ridged sneakers and hiking boots that deposit bits of dirt filled with microbes that make change inevitable.

We pass a cluster of black birds with huge red-balloon chests. "They are frigate birds, the pirates of the islands. Oho, look at them!" Pablo points us skyward where two black birds, like bomber planes, go after a smaller, graceful beige bird until a fish drops from its mouth. "Got it!" Pablo yells in delight as the black frigate scoops the fish before it hits the water.

Pablo sounds like a little boy, still full of the pleasure of these wildlife dramas after twelve years as a guide. A biology major in college, he speaks English perfectly, which he attributes to an English wife and mother, but as I look at his piercing black eyes, black mustache, and pirate beard, I think of the conquistadors riding with Francisco Pizzaro to conquer this world for Spain.

Pablo turns back to the frigates who sit quietly, red chests bursting. "They aren't killers, just thieves." He smiles. "Now they are waiting to mate." That's why their red pouches, tucked away during food hunting, are in full view. The bigger the red pouch, the more sexually attractive they are. I'm thinking of the bulging breasts in bikinis: same technique, only they were pale and covered in sunblock.

Back on the beach, fifty feet from our *panga,* a sleek sea lion approaches, a five-hundred-pounder, honking like a goose. "He's showing off!" Pablo says, "He's letting us know that this is his harem and his territory." Each bull stakes out about seventy feet of beachfront as his territory, patrolling twenty or more females that lounge around. We back away, a few steps only, and everyone's happy. On Seymour Island, at least, human and beast have figured life out peacefully.

Across the cove is a small but imposing square-shaped island, like the top of a top hat rising in the water. It is Daphne Major, where two professors, Paul and Rosemary Grant from Princeton University, have been gathering data to prove Darwin's theory for twenty-five years, using computer analysis to study how the beaks of finches affect survival, especially in droughts and floods.

Solid black volcanic rock with sides plunging straight into the rocky surf make this island seem impossible to climb, let alone live on, for six months a year. That's what the Professors Grant and their assistants do, bringing in all the gear and water they'll need. Their description of arriving, which I read on the plane with incredulity in Jonathan Weiner's Pulitzer Prize–winning book, *The Beak of the Finch*, now seems believable:

> The first one off the panga has to leap when a swell lifts the boat to the top of this ledge, which has the surface area of a large welcome mat. Often the panga will be flying up above the welcome mat a few meters, then dropping down below the mat a few meters, or more, depending on the mood of the ocean ("miscalled Pacific," as Darwin notes in his Beagle diary—for it is not always as calm as it is this morning). From the panga the ledge seems to shoot up as high as a ceiling and then plummet as deep as a basement.

Our sea, so far, is calm, with only a gentle roll, no basement-to-attic swells. A few faces do look green after lunch, including Eleanor's, who says her Thermaderm patch has always worked before. "I get carsick on a curvy road without it," she says, lying flat on the deck now, eyes shut, so she can't see the waves. She tells me about crossing the ocean on the USS *Constitution* once—with three kids under eight—and being sick for five days straight in her cabin. "Worst time of my life."

"So why on Earth pick a boat trip?" I ask, holding back a laugh. The Galapagos was her idea. I would have been happy doing nature on solid land, like in Costa Rica.

"I thought the patches would work!" Eleanor says, smiling with eyes still shut.

I'm thinking I should offer my wristbands—I feel fine—until I remember Uncle Sol's fishing boat and my head over the railing all day. I rethink Darwin: Natural selection may depend on wristbands.

Whenever we hit land to hike or water to snorkel, Eleanor perks up, and so does Louise from Dallas, who is prone and pale green nearby. Neither complains. "The complainers are on cruise ships," says Louise, who went on several cruises before her husband died; now she's switched to small eco-tours. "If you sign up for this boat, you don't expect perfection," she says, turning a shade greener. "You just hang in there."

That's what I tell myself as we wiggle into wet suits, snorkel masks, liners, and fins and coat ourselves with sunblock to snorkel in the freezing ocean. I'm a lake and pool swimmer, not used to fish surprises sneaking up on me, but I am fine among angel and parrot fish in twos and fours. And among a school of yellow stripes, acting as if I'm not there. And even with the manta ray hugging the ocean bottom (Pablo has dived thirty feet on his own lung power to point it out). But when Pablo points out two white sharks, which he calls "friendly," I head toward the *panga*, ready to get out. Unfortunately what looks like two barracudas are between me and the *panga* driver; so I return to the middle of the snorkelers—Where's Stu? He's disappeared—and look for his bloody leg to float by. "Trumpet fish," says Pablo, later, when I show him the picture of my barracudas in the guidebook. Not to worry.

We are to sleep in a six-foot cabin with bunk beds, while the *Samba* motors to the southernmost islands, nearer to Antarctica.

"This isn't for honeymooners!" I joke to Stu, who looks surprisingly green. He's the one with the iron stomach, but I have the magic wristbands, which he refused to bring. "Do you want mine?" I ask, hoping his stubbornness will make him say no.

"No!"

"Don't be so stubborn," I say, and bump my head getting into the bottom bunk while he, climbing in above me, warns not to do anything fancy, like sitting up.

I wonder about squeezing in beside him—no way, unless we lie on our sides all night—so I imagine myself back in the cradle instead. That is what Pablo recommends when sleeping on a boat. I try to hold this image as we rock, roll and Time drifts away and back again, like surf on sand. My wristbands (God bless Chinese acupressure technology) keep working, so I come on deck my normal color, ready for breakfast, and meet Eleanor and Louise, who both slept on the open deck, under the stars. It was grand, they said. No, not cold at all. Stu nods, says he's fine, too, but he skips the mango pancakes in favor of ocean spray.

143

"Maybe I'll find a man," says Rhona, the California divorcée, and Abby, the twelve-year-old, giggles. We are on La Plaza, where the bachelor sea lions hang out. The bachelors are waiting to grow enough to take over a harem, and there will be plenty of opportunities. The bulls, on twenty-four-hour patrol duty, have no time to eat. They service all their females on an empty stomach, shedding pounds until, thin and weak, stronger bulls overpower them. Then they go to the sea for an eating binge of three or four weeks, return to take over a harem and beachfront, and the cycle begins again. They all are happy, especially the females of the harem, who, unlike modern women, get to loll around every day with a hot male and no list of things to do. Pablo points to a platform of volcanic rock made shiny as marble from use. It's where the bulls sleep with their mates, and Rhona and I lie down on it for a photo op of the easy life.

On the cliffs above the bulls, two blue-footed boobies are courting. We stand around to watch as each one lifts its four-toed, webbed foot for the other in a mating dance. "We should try that," says the California "newlywed" (under five years is new by my standards) to his wife, looking inventive enough to make even those bunk beds work.

"Oooh, they are sooo cute," coos twelve-year-old Abby.

"Maybe I'll learn a few tricks," quips Rhona, who may well be the biggest predator on these islands. She likes Pablo. She likes the captain. She likes Walter, the cook—and so do I, but I've had a two-hundred-pound bull named Stu on my patrol since 1961. The boobies keep dancing, people keep joking, and I am feeling like a voyeur. Are we here only to watch sex, or what? When the group moves on, I hold back, enjoying the silence and how the black clouds light up on the horizon.

Espaniola, the next day, looks barren as the moon, except for white bird droppings covering the rocks. "That stuff is essential," Pablo says, "so the boobies and swallowtail gulls can cool off." Without it, the black lava rock becomes unbearably hot, even at 9:00 A.M., as we are discovering. I put on extra sunblock, offer it around.

Up the rocky path we are trailed by mockingbirds, a Galapagos variety. They have long beaks that come within an inch of my water bottle, no shyness here. But we are told, for natural selection's sake, to give them nothing, not a drop.

Not a drop makes me think of "The Rime of the Ancient Mariner" and having to memorize "Water, water, everywhere, and not a drop to drink" for senior English. We are waiting to see the albatross. In Coleridge's poem it was the holy bird, which the mariner killed and was punished with hot, becalmed seas. As penance he had to wear the bird around his neck:

> Ah, well a day! what evil looks
> Had I from old and young!
> Instead of the cross, the Albatross
> About my neck was hung.

It is a true story, according to local legend, and happened not far from here. "But there were two boats, not one," says Pablo. "The one killed the Albatross for food and no one survived. The other didn't and was saved to tell the tale, which Coleridge then heard in England."

We are at the edge of the meadow where the albatross comes yearly to court and mate, ten thousand couples, monogamous for life. I identify with my fellow anomalies on-marriage-one and holding. Nothing appears. Raymond, the California newlywed, is restless, shuffling back and forth on his feet, his digital camera ready to shoot and then show us the results that night on the computer he brought from home. The rest of us are sitting on sharp rocks, fending off thirsty mockingbirds, dozing. I am trying to have a dead-looking bush make a shadow on me. The sun is so hot.

> There passed a weary time. Each throat
> Was parched, and glazed each eye.
> A weary, weary time!

Eventually I hear clicking. It is not the digital camera but beaks clicking like castanets, and then two albatross come from behind the bushes on the far side of the meadow. "Now we will see the dance," says Pablo, but fifteen minutes later, with us still watching, they appear for only a second before making themselves comfortable in the tall grass. That's it. We can leave.

The librarian mother I now know as Kate tells me that Big Bird on Sesame Street is based on the albatross. I like a nobler image, a twosome swooping over the cliff, committed for better or worse. We hurry down the trail, Stu taking my elbow, as everyone tries to reach our boat before the sun sets and the sea blackens with no moon.

145

We are getting into the rhythms of these islands. On sea our bodies lean into the rolls with less struggle. Stu's appetite is back. I have lent my wristbands to Eleanor, who is feeling better and has now lent them to Louise, who for lunch has just finished a plate of fish and is smiling. On land fewer cameras click. Everyone feels less need to capture every animal on film, and we are quieter between joking, absorbing the pleasures of nature's silence.

But I need more, I tell myself, in order not to go to Devil Crown, where Pablo promises great snorkeling among big fish.

"More sharks?" I ask.

"Why not!" His black eyes dance with challenge.

"Come on!" Stu says, handing me my gear. "Don't be a scaredy-cat. I need company."

I look at the gray sky, white caps, and ominous thirty-foot rocks that we are headed for and say, "So stay with me." He zips up his suit—Real men can't be wimps here—and I am left with the woman with my sun hat. She is seventy-two, a widow. "I'm too old for such cold water," says Edith, ready to talk, but I am ready to wash off my pangs of cowardice in a hot shower and write postcards of adventure, with the whole upper deck to myself.

We have come to see Lonesome George. He is the last surviving giant tortoise of his sub-species and lives in the Darwin Research Center, which houses him and other endangered species of the Galapagos. They keep presenting him with possible mates, to no avail so far, but not to worry, says Pablo. He's only 60 and can live to 150. We spot Lonesome George under a shade bush near the pond where his betrothed is taking a dip. Inch by inch she heads toward him, causing Abby to give off her usual "Sooo adorable!" Adorable is a stretch when you are looking at a grim-faced, 550-pound hulk in need of a face lift. Imagine E.T. without a smile. In fact E.T. was inspired by this face. "Spielberg was down here," says Pablo. Stu wants me to crouch next to Lonesome George. "Move a little closer." I do. "Closer, like you want to give him a hug." I laugh, he clicks, and I am already imagining this story and the one about how the next time I see these creatures swimming by me in the sea, I'll be cool.

They are standing on one foot, very still. Five flamingos in shrimp pink. The color comes from eating shrimp, in fact. They are the bright spot in a landscape of mud grays and browns highlighted only by a glassy stillness under a flat gray sky. Nothing moves, not even a ripple of the brackish water that continually seeps in from the sea. I decide that the flamingo stands on one long foot to keep his pink belly clean, for with the weight of two feet, the crusted edges of lagoon would give way. Our twelve-year-old Abby finds that out, as she heads toward them and the mirrored water. "Go on!" Pablo urges.

"Oooh," she squeals, as with each step more of her feet disappears.

Pablo rolls back his head and laughs, so we assume safety, not quicksand. "Go on, go on!" And we join in until, knee-high, Abby's had enough and, slower than a giant tortoise, returns, holding up her Teva sandals hidden by mud. Everyone laughs, snapping photos—until a sulfuric smell makes us back away. "Nothing bad," Pablo says, looking like a pirate with his head wrapped in a pink-and-red bandanna. "It's like your California mud baths. She'll just have a rash for a few minutes." Abby's skin turns prickly red under the smelly mud, but no one is reaching into a backpack of "what ifs," no one offers cortisone ointment or bacitracin, just in case. Abby races back down the trail to the turquoise sea, and we move slowly forward, smiling.

The sun, from one minute to the next, has reappeared. The sky is now a China blue, and the heat has put me in a snorkeling mood. The sea lions lounge on the sand, glossy with wetness, others play in the water, and Marty spots two penguins sunning on the rocks. A rare sight, this special Galapagos penguin which prefers the equator to the ice floes of Antarctica.

"Hurry, hurry," Pablo says. "We can swim with them!"

We race to the *panga*, race to the *Samba*, change quickly, and are in the icy water fifteen minutes later, feeling delicious. We see stingrays, a good-sized squid, parrot fish, and several sea turtles bobbing their heads above the surface nearby. But no sea lions come to play and no sign of penguins—until suddenly a dozen charge, swimming in between us like bullets, and then they are gone. The younger women squeal in joy, and I adjust my mask, pleased.

"White-tipped sharks!" Abby shouts with glee, and I see them, four of them, to my right far below me. I don't squeal, but I don't hail the *panga* to get me out of here either. Yes, I am brave enough to come back alive. Yes.

Tap, tap, tap. A nightly sound as California Raymond taps away at his computer, and we all await the results. He is feeding the pictures, which are being readied to post on his home page, from his digital cam-

era into his laptop, as we cluster around him. OOOhhh, there's the flamingo on one foot! we say in awe, but Raymond is disappointed with
the blank white sky. "No problem," he says, and uses his Photo Editor
to add pink and blue. He moves his wife, Cory, closer to the masked
boobie with its chick in the next shot. He says he might have her swim
with the sea lion, too, though now the bull is alone in the scene.

Virtual reality. Not only the vicarious substitute for experience, but
also a maker of experience. I am shocked. You can't trust photos anymore. In ten years will Raymond and Cory remember that she'd never
swum with sea lions? That it was the penguins that whizzed past? But
then I realize that he is doing with photos what I do with words, making the sky the color I need. I like remembering the pale white blank-
ness above the tiny dot of pink standing on one stick leg, so still. And
then the child holding mud-covered Tevas, the group laughter, the smell
of sulfur, the cleansing in a turquoise sea—if indeed it was turquoise.
I must supply the context to make the experience mine: sometimes with
the bold, black swoop of a Galapagos hawk I see now against blue sky,
or sometimes with a white band of empty sky, or the grace of stillness
and the rolling rhythms that rock me as I write these words.

We are climbing the volcano, straight up into the sun, the wind gusting so hard my big hat feels as if it can become a flying machine. Hundreds of wooden steps have been built above the loose brown dirt that
would slip out from under our feet if we tried to walk on it. "Stay on
the steps," Pablo says, leaping ahead with the under-fifties while we
over-fifties plod skyward. We stop to look at the pioneering lava cacti,
the only thing growing in this arid nothingness. We stop to look at Pinnacle Peak, a tuff cone of dried volcanic ash, like a mini skyscraper in
the cove below. Really we are stopping to catch our breath, but at least
all of us are here: big-hatted, water bottles on hips. Even Edith, at seventy-two, has come. She never thought not to, says this part-time principal of a Sunday school. She plods, one foot, then the other, holding
on to her hat as I do mine. "You can always stop and wait for us to come
down," I tell her.

"Go ahead! Don't wait for me!" she yells over the wind, but we do,
happy for an excuse to hold back for someone else. I study Stu, worrying as always about his heart, and want to tell him what I told Edith:
Wait down below.

No way. Not even worth a hint. Climbing this volcano in hot sun,
straight up, with no comment, is why he is here twelve years after his

heart attack—though he didn't know that when we signed up. It's like me swimming with sharks, and why Edith, ten minutes after we all reached the top, arrives, and we cheer and take snapshots of the whole group under the sign, "Bartolome: 0 degrees, 20 seconds" meaning we're exactly, well almost, on the equator (minus twenty seconds, which is one-third of a degree). Below us Pinnacle Rock, formidable from the sea, looks like a skyscraper six inches high.

The last day. The men are fiddling with computerized photos somewhere, the women are on deck watching the captain unfurl the jib sail. He likes to use it for fun, despite the running engine. Rhona says she has gotten what she came for on this trip. "After you look into the crater of a volcano, the dumb things in life don't matter!" She has decided that she need not be in a rut just because she's forty plus and single. She is going to look for a new job, join the Sierra Club, and keep traveling. Edith has also gotten what she wanted: to see if she could rough it, if she could do without her bathtub for a week. "I climbed a volcano at seventy-two, in the hot sun," she beams. "I can't believe I swam with sharks," I say, which is what I wrote on every postcard home. Eleanor and Louise are eating nuts and drinking margaritas, as the boat rocks.

"I'm forty-eight and swam with a giant sea turtle," says Kate, the quiet librarian, ecstatic. "And that's why I'm here with my daughter, so she won't have to wait thirty-six years to do the same!"

Our Abby blushes at her mother's enthusiasm. I nod. Rhona smiles. Edith takes off her hat—and we all decide to lie on the deck, in the last rays of sun, without any sunblock on.

Gradually Grandma

When the operator interrupted my phone call so Julie could say, "How'd you like to be a grandma?" I said, "So fast?" I thought I had more time. Forget that I'd been mooning at the Baby Gap window for years—and that my mother had been forty and I'd be fifty-seven when that name would apply. Grannies were little old ladies in sensible shoes, and I wore boots with platform heels.

Nor was I ready to be put on a pedestal of grandmotherly wisdom, and on the first day of questions, I fell right off. What did you do for heartburn? Did you have an amneo? Did you eat unprocessed cheese like Brie? How about bologna with nitrates? Either I didn't remember, was too embarrassed to say, or didn't know what Julie was talking about.

Thirty-four years ago I was twenty-three, and my mother was a thousand miles away when I carried Julie. If there were books on babies (aside from Dr. Spock's), I'd never heard of them. I drank, smoked (my son thinks he'd be two inches taller if I hadn't), ate everything, and never knew I was supposed to play Mozart and read Dr. Seuss out loud nightly to educate the fetus. There wasn't even Lamaze in our town. Having a baby meant deciding between two kinds of shots to dull the pain, and although breast-feeding was sort of in, so was Similac formula. So were baby-sitters, who let me escape to see "Tom Jones" three times and to not hear Julie, who screamed with colic every night from eight until after midnight. I used to love telling that story—how I kept asking Stu in the dark, quiet theater, "Can't we stay here? See it again?" It was what I remembered best, but that wasn't what future grandmothers were supposed to tell their daughters about the joys of parenting. Especially if the daughter had been working nonstop for years and was used to drinking wine and eating Brie cheese to her heart's delight.

Despite my shaky start, Julie called to see if I wanted to go to Goldfinger's, a discount store in Newark, to help her buy baby furniture.

"So soon?" I asked.

"Absolutely," Julie said, "it takes ages to deliver."

"As long as it takes to have a baby?" I laughed. She did not.

"You don't have to go, Mom, if you don't want to." Her voice sounded somber. "Marg is coming."

"Of course I'll come." Marg is Julie's mother-in-law, and her daughter had a baby already. I'd be damned if I'd let them go without me, even if all I remembered about baby furniture was buying a crib and dresser at the last minute off the floor of the nearest store around.

"Great! I'll send you the list."

"The list?"

"Yes, so you can advise me, okay?" The list, it turned out, was four pages long and included: fifteen items under Nursery, fourteen under Bedding, nineteen under Layette, seventeen under Baby Needs, seventeen under On the Go, fourteen under Bon Appétit, six under Hanging Out, twelve under Fun Time, and eleven empty spaces to fill in under Odds and Ends. This was like going to summer camp, I joked, but only to Stu.

Goldfinger's looked like a tiny dump from the outside—We actually traveled an hour for this???—but inside sprawled a whole city block of more merchandise than any mega store in a mall. There must have been hundreds of crib and dresser sets, fifteen stroller styles and carriages, a wall of car seats, two rooms worth of layettes, twenty nursing gliders (rocking chairs that glided). Astounding. The only thing I recognized was a small plastic infant seat I'd used with both kids, and it had a sign, "Last one— $3.99!" Five hours later we staggered into the light, after having ordered "the basics." Mission accomplished, and we three were still talking.

I can play this grandma role, I thought, euphoric, as I climbed into my car. I was forever grateful to my friend with three daughters-turned-mothers, who gave me the magic words. I used them when asked if a glider is better than a rocker and if a dressing table should flip down or slide out on top of the dresser: *Whatever you feel comfortable with!* I even used them after I said that I liked white better than natural wood, so did Marg, and Julie said she liked natural wood best. So we both said, "Whatever you feel most comfortable with." Marg, as I mentioned earlier, already had a daughter-turned-mother.

"So what do you think, Mom? When should I call you?" It is month nine and we are having lunch together in an outdoor café a block from Julie's office. She's working two more weeks and is swamped, she says. I don't say what Stu and I worry about nightly, "You're working too hard." I am eating chicken in wild mushrooms and Julie is eating a bowl of plain penne, and I don't say, "You have to eat for two. You need energy." She isn't hungry, she says, but most of the pasta is gone. I don't make a joke about that, so you see how I've improved. "So when should I call you?"

"When?"

"When I'm having the baby."

"Oh, definitely call us." I'm thinking of Doug calling from a hospital pay phone, "It's a boy!"—to be Matthew or Jason—or "It's Carly Rose!" That name is definite, after Stu's father and mother and also Carly Simon.

"Even in the middle of the night?"

She looks like the child we sent to camp, asking when we will come back for her. I swallow a glib "Hey, this is your baby not mine!" and even a milder "How about after breakfast?"

"Whatever you feel comfortable with!" I see a big smile. "But you could," I take a bite of chicken to stall, "wait until you are sure you are *staying* in the hospital before we come. There is false labor, you know."

I want to tell her that I had it for a week with her—that we went to the hospital twice in dead winter and once we had a flat coming home, that we were out there in ten-below weather, contractions and hard kicks still coming every now and then, that I was shining a flashlight for half an hour so Stu could get the bolts off and on. But that was an after-the-birth story.

"Was Grandma there when you were in labor?"

"I think so. She and Grandpa were definitely there when you were born." I try to think of an upbeat story about that, but all I remember is a terrible snowstorm and being in labor for twenty-two hours, so that even though it took them eight hours instead of two to arrive, they had plenty of time to sit around. "Luckily we only live an hour away," I say lamely, thinking I'm failing the grandma test again. "Sure, call me at 3 A.M., if you want."

"How long until you gave me a bottle?" I keep chewing. All I remember is that my breasts were not satisfying and I panicked, switched to a bottle. Was it three days, a week? Either way, I shelve that one.

"How about some dessert? Fruit salad?"

"I'm fine." Julie looks at her watch. She has to get back and edit her story, and I have to take my mother to the foot doctor on the other side of town.

"The one thing I do remember is my awe, just looking at you. How this tiny, tiny thing came out of me—and Dad, of course! It was such a miracle. I didn't feel that until I actually held you in my arms, terrified of course, because I knew absolutely nothing of babies. But you survived my care."

"I did," she laughs, and I think, Bingo! I've done good. I had sensed she'd been thinking, Can I do this? Will I be good? Not to mention the identity questions, which I didn't have then. Should she stay home? How long? Who will she be now? Mother? Career woman? At twenty-three I wasn't anybody yet, and who I was to become, aside from wife and mom, was years away.

I am still trying to figure that out, this time as Grandma, but I am more used to not knowing. Would I baby-sit twice a week like my re-tired colleague who goes to Philadelphia on Thursdays to watch her granddaughter and to Manhattan on Mondays to watch a new grand-son? "You've become a professional nanny," I kid her. "You'd have less work if you'd kept teaching biology!" Would I ever, like my neighbor, spend three weeks of every month with daughter and granddaughter, three hours away? "She just comes home to do her laundry," the aban-doned husband told me at a recent party, stuffing himself with hummus and pita as if he hadn't eaten all week.

My mother baby-sat for a week when Julie was nine months old. I could do that. My mother-in-law played tirelessly with Julie and Alan with nonstop pleasure. I didn't know about that. I thought of our ex-hausted neighbors, staggering down the street after they took their three grandchildren home after a two-week stay. Wonderful, wonder-ful, they said, but they could hardly make the steps to their house.

"Would you like to go to Barnes and Noble and buy some books on birth and babies?" I ask Julie as I pay the bill. (Maybe there's one for grandmas with platform heels, too.) I want books that make childbirth no problem, just a natural act. That was the thought that saved me: This is how it's supposed to be. You'll survive this, everyone else has.

"Thanks, Mom, but I have to get back. I start editing my segment in ten minutes." She pats her belly, which she doesn't hide in over-sized smocks as I did. "It's about women's magazines and their promises for a perfect body. Right, huh?" She laughs, smoothing her red T-shirt to show every kick. I had seen the magazines stacked in her office when I came to pick her up: "Ten Ways to Great Thighs," "What Flat Stomachs Can Do for Sex," "Breast Appeal and How to Get It." I had thought, wow, she's feeling insecure. I was wrong again.

I watch her heave out of her chair, head for the street, hail me a taxi, and march purposely up the block toward her office, which she'll do for another week, Junior leading the way out front. I imagine her cutting and rearranging snippets of interviews and headlines about good thighs, good sex, and whatever else women are told they should do for success.

Then I remember her holding a beer bottle at a picnic when she was four months old, and climbing to the top of the jungle gym at two, and yelling "higher, higher" to anyone pushing her swing, and telling her father, "Sit down right here, Daddy," a producer at age four, wanting him to color with her. The good memories rush back, like water into tide pools, and I keep looking at this child who came out of me, fast-walking my future grandchild across 65th Street, into the crowd. I am still in awe.

In a House by a Lake

The birds woke me—not the shifting of the mattress or a command to turn over. And last night no one said, "What are you doing?" as Stu says when, sleepless, I get up to take a bath in the middle of the night. But last night I didn't get up. I slept through, as I have all week in this little brown house at the end of the dirt road where huge pines loom.

I'm surprised, for I do not know this house on Fernwood Point. Stu and I slept here together for only a few nights before he left for a conference, and now I'm on my own, knowing where nothing is, how nothing works. I, who am vigilant against leaky sinks and new wall cracks at home in New Jersey, look only at how the New Hampshire winds lightly shift the lake's surface, drawing me into its rhythms. I do not pick up the telephone; I do not even turn on the radio.

Maybe it's the coziness of rooms I do not rattle around in, rooms without memories, easy to manage. I could clean the whole place in twenty minutes. I could retrieve whatever I left in the furthest corner in thirty seconds. Best of all, in this house of bargains and discards rescued for a new start, I could start again, and without obligations for perfection this time. A curved brown sofa, discontinued model, four creaky, cane chairs from the attic, a cookie sheet doubling as a tray, a bathtub in the bedroom, lounge chairs that let you sink to the springs all whisper, "Don't bother about us! All is fine!"

Maybe it's the freedom from "Where's the mustard?" or from instructions to "Take the film in, and get four-by-sixes, not three-by-fives this time!" Peck, peck, peck, like a bird feeding on tossed grain. I love the silence. Yesterday, before sunset, I bolted for the harbor, ate a frozen yogurt with chocolate sprinkles as the sky turned purple, and came home to leftover wonton soup with noodles that had turned pink from the pork strips. I finished with a raw carrot and mint tea. Delicious—and without anyone's comment on the order of things.

Maybe it's how the morning sun lights the stillness and how the breeze blows ripples against the beach while I sip coffee on a wobbly redwood bench. And how a sudden storm can whip up the waves and how lightning ignites the black sky. I watch for an hour, my face pressed close to the window, as I imagine myself on the beach's edge, my body soaked, my arms raised in a dare. Try me. I will be fearless. And so what if there is a direct hit on the white birch, angled over the dock, our only shade. It does not split in two; only a small branch is cracked, dangling there.

Maybe it's because when the sun returns, I can picture my grand-child on the tiny beach, playing with a small, blue pail left by someone. It is filled with sea shells, and she is lifting them out, one by one, as her curled toes dig into warm sand until she flings them as far as she can, assuming they will float back. And if not, she—or he—won't care. The circles widening across the glassy surface stretching toward Mount Kearsage will be enough.

Maybe it's because the child in me no longer listens for robbers and forgets how she would play dead for hours, waiting for the end. Here the thuds against the dock, the cracking of branches, the moonlight fading and returning on the whim of clouds seem free of what ifs. And if a water pipe bursts or if the power fails, there's a flashlight somewhere, and if that doesn't work, I will stumble my way to bed and go to sleep early, wrapped in a blanket of come what may.

Maybe it's because if I'm awake at midnight, I will swim with or without a moon, cold or not, and no one will say, "Don't!" I will swim past the neighbors' docks with long arms ready to rescue, past the old wooden boathouse with its sign, "Beware of Thin Ice," and head for the Point, where crosscurrents pull and push me, demanding that I let myself be carried—not on my back but treading water without intent, gathering strength for the return.

Stu calls from New Jersey for the second time today to read me last night's fortune cookie: Your sweetheart may be too beautiful for words but not for argument. We laugh, for the arguing is what we both don't miss. Every day, it's exhausting work to decide who left the shower dripping and who bought the no-fat instead of low-fat yogurt. These are substitutes for the big arguments about money, children, neglect, and betrayal I heard on NPR this morning—yes, the radio is on again! Petty bickering means equality, said the romance expert with the new book. "The hero and heroine always take each other on in chitchat *before* they fall in love." And *afterward*, too, I would add, because we keep needing to draw lines of turf in our shared sand, even as they blow away.

I tell Stu about the black bear I saw crossing the highway and about Buzz and Edie, who were floating on tire rafts two docks down; they've been coming here for thirty-five years. And how I made blueberry pancakes as if I were serving both of us. The recipe makes twelve pancakes, but you can't halve an egg, so I've had pancakes for three mornings—and blueberries, too sour alone, were so delicious in batter.

I will make more, I say, when he comes home, and I have signed up for tennis. I cup the phone in the crook of my neck, whispering, "I miss you"—and suddenly I do, as if I were again the girl waiting for Saturday night with the boy from bio lab who liked my curves and me.

How easy aloneness is when I assume it will end at the airport tomorrow at 6:05 P.M., standing at gate three, sporting a new haircut that he'd better notice and say, "You look great!" And if he doesn't because it's hot and the plane is an hour late, he will still nudge my neck and whisper, "I always love that smell!" And we won't argue about that—or about anything—as long as I've closed the car windows and put the photographs he wanted developed on the kitchen table next to the mail.

Acknowledgments

First my thanks to my husband, Stu, for listening to years of early drafts about us before his second cup of coffee—and to my children, Julie and Alan, and my mother for their input and continued goodwill about my take on their lives. I am also grateful to the many generous readers who helped me shape this manuscript, especially Max Apple, Andrea Cooper, Mimi Danson, Stephen Dunn, Penny Dugan, Carolyn Jackson, Betty Lies, Joyce Lott, Scotia MacRae, Nancy Sommers, Mike Steinberg, Gail Ullman, and members of the U.S.1 Poets' Cooperative. Finally, my thanks to staff of the University of Nebraska Press for their advice, good humor, and support in making this book happen.

I would also like to thank the editors of the following publications, in which these essays first appeared: "Front Door on the Driveway" (summer 1993), "A Map to Cape Cod" (spring 1999), and "Improvisation on 'I Do'" (spring 2000) in *Puerto del Sol*; "Sewing Lesson" in *Princeton Arts Review*, summer 1996; "Closet Fantasies" in *Philadelphia Inquirer Magazine*, 27 March 1994; "Negotiating Monogamy" in *Pennsylvania English*, fall 2001; "Weighing In between Rubens and Modigliani" in *The New Press Literary Quarterly*, summer/fall 1995; "The Power of the Cap" in *Brevity*, fall 1999; "Trudging the Towpath for Therapy" (retitled "Towpath Therapy") in *Times of Trenton*, 27 September 1998; "The Mortar of Tradition" (retitled "A Night for Haroset") in *Jewish Week*, April 1990, and in CALYX: *A Journal of Art and Literature by Women* 20, no. 1 (winter 2001); "Living with Loss, Dreaming of Lace" (retitled "Dreaming of Lace") in *Lear's Magazine*, October 1990; "Stress Test" (spring 1994), "No One Ever Told Me about Jimmy and June" (retitled "Jimmy and June") (spring 1995), "Cappuccino at Rosa's" (spring 1996), "Doorknob Conviction" (fall 1998), and "There's Always the Afternoon" (spring 1999) in *U.S. 1 Worksheets*; "Changing Lanes" in *The Fourth Genre*, spring 2001; "Tomboyhood Revisited" in *Kelsey Review*, summer 1995; "Anonymous Translation" in *Florida Review*, summer 1999; "If and When" in *Creative Nonfiction*, fall 1993; "Game Plan," copyright 2000, from *Wise Women: Reflections of Teachers at Midlife*, ed. Phyllis R. Freeman and Jan Zlotnik Schmidt (New York: Routledge, 2000) ; reproduced by permission of Taylor & Francis, Inc., *http://www.routledge.ny.com*; "In Glorietta Canyon" in *Coastal Forest Review*, fall 1994; "The Other Redhead and Me" in *Living on the Margins: Women Writers on Breast Cancer*, ed. Hilda Raz (New York: Persea, 1999).

In the American Lives series

Thoughts from a Queen-Sized Bed
by Mimi Schwartz

Phantom Limb
by Janet Sternburg